MAKE YOUR OWN
RUGS
A GUIDE TO DESIGN AND TECHNIQUE

MAKE YOUR OWN
RUGS

A GUIDE TO DESIGN AND TECHNIQUE

SUE PEVERILL

HAMLYN

Title page: Dilys Stinson's "Blue Salmon".
This flat-weave tapestry rug was very clearly
inspired by the paintings of Klee, Kandinsky and
other great modern artists.

First published 1989 by The Hamlyn
Publishing Group Limited, a division
of The Octopus Publishing Group,
Michelin House, 81 Fulham Road,
London SW3 6RB

Produced by Justin Knowles Publishing Group
9 Colleton Crescent, Exeter, Devon EX2 4BY

Designed by Ron Pickless

Typeset by Keyspools Ltd, Golborne, Lancashire

ISBN 0 600 564 967

Produced by Mandarin Offset
Printed and bound in Hong Kong

Contents

INTRODUCTION

The number of artists and designers who are discovering the design and making of rugs as a creative and exciting medium through which to express their ideas is huge, but more than matched by the astonishing diversity of their finished products. Moreover, these finished products are available from an ever-increasing number of outlets, some traditional and others newer and more specialized.

The popularity of rug design as a medium in which to express artistic ideas is part of the growing general enthusiasm for the applied arts, which are currently enjoying a renaissance stimulated by a renewed interest in and awareness of the possibilities of good individual design, whether the medium be textiles, rugs, furniture or ceramics. This renaissance is being further encouraged by a large number of magazines devoted entirely to interior design and in Britain by the work of such bodies as the Crafts Council and the Design Council, which promote and support excellence in all fields of the applied arts and design.

This awareness by modern rug makers of the importance of design is perhaps the most important reason why the status of rugs, and more specifically of designed rugs, has been raised from the slough in which it languished for at least 30 years. Indeed, until about the end of the 1970s the prevalent image of rug design was one of a rather well intentioned but essentially dull worthiness that expressed itself in texture at the expense of form and design. All that has changed in recent years. While many contemporary rug designers are fully aware and appreciative of ethnic and traditional weaving techniques – so that they can use them as part of their repertoire should the right occasion arise – it is the *reinterpretation* of past ideas and traditions that is proving such a vital stimulus for the present.

Alongside the traditionally trained weavers there are countless artists and designers who are approaching rug design from quite different disciplines – painting, for example, or printed-textile design, furniture making, ceramics, murals . . . the list could go on for a long time. A major source of inspiration for some artists has been the interior decoration, textiles and furniture born from the austerity of the 1930s and 1940s in combination with the science/technology vision of the more prosperous post-war period. A very noticeable influence has been the work of the Cubist painters, whose abstract shapes and exciting use of colour first inspired E. McKnight Kauffer and Marian Dorn in the 1930s to produce a series of designs that revolutionized rug making, freeing it from the traditional constraints of the patterned border and the staid oriental motifs which had

Hand-knotted rug by Betty Joel, made in China about 1937 using a Persian knot with mixed fibres (mainly wool) on undyed cotton. Further to highlight the simple geometric design, a groove has been cut in the pile around the thick and thin lines and the red circle.

enjoyed such pre-eminence during the Victorian era. More recently, the influence of Miró, Klee, Kandinsky and Matisse has become very evident in the boldness of colour and richness of form employed by modern rug designers – to the extent that, to choose a single example, Liz Kitching's 1984 "Miróesque" rugs were a direct homage to the painter, translating the spirit and exuberance of his paintings into the medium of the rug.

The visual art of the past is such a rich source of inspiration that it is impossible to ignore; rather than attempt to do so, many contemporary rug makers find it more fruitful to be aware of its influence and actively incorporate its ideas into their own designs. Nevertheless, while it is a truism that nothing in the field of design is ever totally

Hand-knotted rug by Ronald Grierson, made in India in 1935. It has a mainly wool pile, using a Persian knot, on a cotton warp and a mixed weft. In this design Grierson acknowledged the work of the Cubist painters, with his Cubist-style motifs worked in brown, black and cream on a pinkish-beige background.

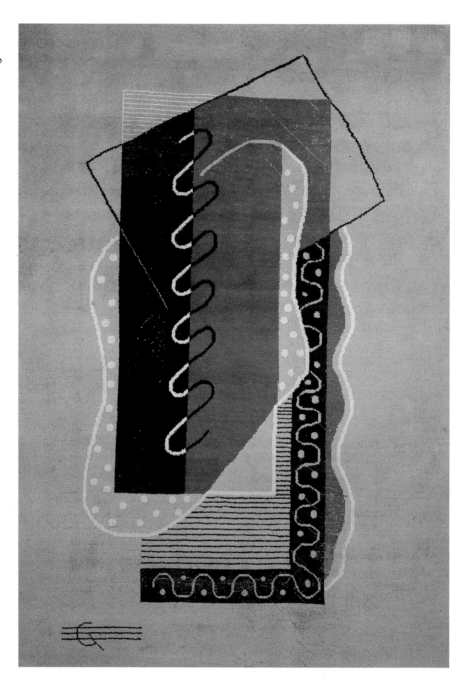

original, there is much in rug making that is fresh and innovative. For example, Julia Burrowes, who studied as a painter and who has a deep love of the works of the Impressionists, has in her rug making used the pointillist approach to great effect (see pages 48–50). She takes clumps of colour and shading outwards, thereby producing a subtle effect that appears to outline a pattern more and more strongly as you move further away from the rug.

Julia works mainly in the field of rag rugs, and so her painterly technique is not always immediately obvious: traditionally, rag rugs have explored more the possibilities of texture than of visual design. By contrast, rugs that are gun-tufted can achieve an effect that closely mirrors the sweep of a painter's brush-stroke. The tufting gun's rapid-fire delivery of yarn is particularly effective in producing sharply defined and dramatic images on canvas, so that the final result is the nearest thing possible to a painting produced in textiles. An excellent example of the use of this technique is to be found in the rugs of Malcolm Temple (see pages 98–102). His designs have hard, bright edges and a powerful use of primary colour to describe large geometric and abstract shapes that echo the work of Kandinsky and Delauney.

Most rug makers work alone. Their rugs progress much as paintings do, and often take many weeks – if not months – to complete (this is especially true of weaving and allied techniques). The similarity between rug making and painting is in fact a very close one, the differences between them becoming evident only when a rug designer is fulfilling a commission and thus has to operate within the parameters of the client's requirements. The designer has to cope not just with the straightforward stipulations of the assignment – which may specify the use of certain colours and textures, and insist on the incorporation of various motifs, logos or architectural details – but also with considerations such as where the rug will eventually be placed, the availability there of light and space, and the general "feel" and style of that interior. Unless these factors are taken into account, the client – whatever he or she may have stated in the original instructions – will feel somehow short-changed and the work as a whole will anyway be poorly balanced for its environment. In short, a commissioned painting can be expected to mould and enhance the nature of its surroundings, but a commissioned rug must be designed to fit in with and complement them.

Today we are entering a new phase of the design revolution, as the

A woollen pile rug designed by Marian Dorn and made by the Royal Wilton Company in 1937. This rug has a semi-figurative design of wheat-ears in blues, greys and light brown on a cream background.

high-tech look of blacks and greys gives way to a softer, more decorated feel. There is a move towards a personal, individual style, in which the old is mixed eclectically with the contemporary. This applies equally to offices and homes, as more and more people with an aesthetic interest in interior design opt for the unique ''one-off'' qualities that a designed rug or wall-hanging can bring to any room.

This ability of rug designers and rug makers to work to pre-specified requirements and yet still produce strong individual work is one of the reasons why the use of rugs appeals so much to so many architects and design consultants – not to mention their clients. Today people working in interior design are very likely to recognize the potential a well executed rug or wall-hanging has for enhancing the appearance and ''feel'' of any room, not only because of its obvious decorative qualities but also because it can be used to unite the sometimes disparate elements of even the best designed interior.

In this book we look at the work of some of the best of today's rug designers and makers. All share a sincerely avowed interest in good design and professionally executed rugs, and the wealth of inventive and exciting work which they are producing will undoubtedly serve as a rich source of inspiration for future rug makers.

Also included are descriptions of the basic techniques which these rug makers use in order to express their artistic ideas. Of course, such descriptions can be no more than a short introduction: if you wish to start making rugs there is no substitute for learning by experience – in other words, to start making rugs! The task may seem at first daunting, but in fact all that is really involved is the straightforward selection of a design that will suit the particular technique you wish to employ. Thereafter, informed experimentation will provide you with the spark necessary to help you turn your own creative ideas into reality.

1
THE STORY OF
RUG MAKING

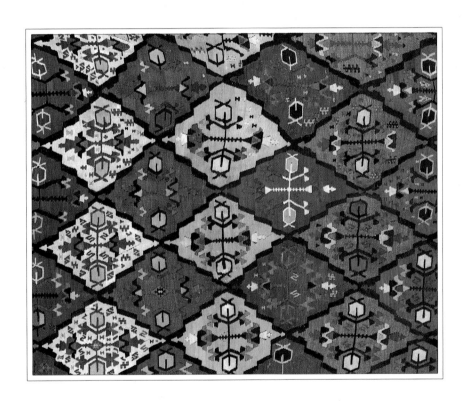

The history of rug making spans many centuries and many cultures. Different cultures and different nations have fostered their own distinctive styles, and these have influenced each other over the centuries. The inevitable pun is that the history of rugs has as many strands as a rug itself. In surveying it, therefore, we have to adopt a culture-by-culture, or country-by-country, approach – while constantly bearing in mind that design ideas permeate across cultural and political boundaries, making themselves felt in often unexpected places.

A Kerman Lavar silk rug inscribed ''Order of Milani, 92''.

The area most usually associated with rug making is the Orient, a vast region ranging eastwards from the Black Sea to China and taking in countries such as Mongolia, Tibet, parts of the Soviet Union, Turkey, Iran, Afghanistan, India, Pakistan, Bangladesh, Egypt and Morocco. With the exceptions of China, India and Tibet, these countries are linked by the common bond of Islam.

A 19th-century Turkish kelim with an interesting, not-quite-repeating motif around the edges. In the central panel it is reversed out in deep reds and blues through beige.

The Mongols

Among the regions associated with China through cultural and political ties are Mongolia, Tibet and the area known as East Turkestan. The Mongols, under Kublai Khan, conquered China in 1206, and during their 150-year occupancy the cultural styles of the invaded and the invaders became irrevocably entwined. The Turkomans of East Turkestan are generally accepted as having a Mongol origin: they themselves have no recorded history of their early days, but the chronicles of Arab historians of the 10th and 11th centuries indicate that the Turkomans were a semi-nomadic people whose main activity was herding sheep. Because of this lifestyle the Turkomans were unable, for obvious reasons, to knit together to form a strong nation, but they nevertheless had a profound cultural effect on those nations with which they came into contact.

The cultural influence of the Mongols spread westwards, too, and nowhere is this more evident than in the art of rug making. It is still a mystery as to when and where the first pile-knotted carpets were made, but all the evidence suggests that the culture responsible was a nomadic one, and hence probably the Mongols. For example, the primary occupation of nomadic peoples is the rearing of sheep as a source of food and, notably, of wool; it is unlikely that in such a society it would have taken long for clothes made of animal pelts to be superseded by garments woven from wool. It is but a short step from woollen garments to woollen rugs.

A major discovery was made in 1947 by a Russian archaeologist called Rudenko. This was a pile-knotted rug which he found in a Scythian burial mound in the Altai Mountains of Siberia, and it dated back to the 5th century BC. The rug was in the same style as much later Oriental productions, having a central field surrounded by borders of varying sizes, the designs on it consisting mainly of animal and floral motifs. Even earlier, during the 1920s, carpet fragments dating from the 2nd and 3rd centuries AD had been excavated at Lou-lan in East Turkestan. Such discoveries add weight to the theory that the making of pile-knotted carpets was an established craft in the Orient long before it came to the west. Certainly pile-knotted rugs were being made in Persia and other parts of the Middle East by the 3rd–5th centuries AD.

Interestingly, the decoration on many ancient pieces corresponds quite closely to that on rugs made during the 19th century, and this suggests that they share a common heritage. It is believed that the link was the presence and cultural influence of the Mongols. Persia was conquered by the Seljuk Turks in the first half of the 11th century, and as a result many parts of that country were colonized by people of Turkish origin who introduced their own culture to the natives. Relevant discoveries of major interest have been made at Konya (the Seljuk capital), Beyshehir and in the ruins of Fostat, Egypt. The rugs found are thought to date back to the 13th century, and are all decorated with the stylized, geometric floral patterns that were still to be in use during the 18th and 19th centuries. There is also a close similarity between these designs and those found on early Mongolian and Chinese fragments.

Another source of influence was Chinese silks. These began to arrive in Persia and Turkey around the 13th century.

Illustrations of rugs abound in manuscripts dating from the 14th century. Most Persian rugs of this era were decorated with stylized geometric patterns, although the incursion of the Mongols introduced a more nature-oriented approach, with designs representing birds, animals and flowers. From the end of the 14th century the Chinese influence became very evident.

Another important factor in the changing design of Persian carpets during the succeeding century was that they were no longer being made by nomads. Persons of influence and power were employing

A Kazakh Karatchop double-ended prayer rug from the late 18th century. The central motif is "boxed in" rather than intertwined and this produces a less rigid effect in the finished design, which is on a shaded blue background.

skilled weavers to practise the art. The motifs they used frequently included blossoms, scrolled leaves, geometric shapes and real and fantastic animals. At the same time, Persian and Turkish rugs were beginning to appear in European paintings. By now the rugs produced in the Imperial factories were being designed by some of the greatest Islamic artists of the age, and rug making was becoming a sophisticated artform. The influx of creative artists to the field resulted in the introduction of new designs which bore little relation to the traditional patterns created in earlier centuries by the nomadic tribes. Rugs and carpets were being commissioned to furnish palaces and important buildings, and had become treasured gifts.

By the middle of the 16th century the European nobility, too, had adopted the habit of commissioning rugs. Motifs popular at the time were medallion designs, garden and hunting scenes, and "vase" carpets. "Vase" carpets are unlike medallion versions in that their pattern is one-way; in other words, if they are looked at from the wrong direction the pattern is upside-down. It is often very difficult to find the vase in a "vase" carpet since frequently it is concealed in a highly complex floral pattern. Such designs of flowers could be merely gratuitous, but very often they were intended as depictions of actual gardens, as we can discover by reading the verses which were frequently incorporated into their borders. Some garden designs, however, used highly stylized geometric forms.

During the 13th and 14th centuries the design of Ottoman rugs was dominated by images of animals and birds – among the more popular themes were heraldic birds, scenes of animals locked in combat, and fantastic beasts. The popularity of such designs decreased during the latter part of the 15th century, and geometric styles became prevalent; one group of rugs designed in this way, using octagonal motifs, is popularly described as the "Holbein carpets", even though they were actually produced about a century before Holbein was painting.

During the 16th and 17th centuries the city of Ushak, Turkey, became an important centre of carpet weaving. Five major types of rugs were produced: double-ended mihrab prayer rugs, star-patterned rugs, medallion rugs, bird carpets and ball-and-line-pattern carpets, the latter two generally being woven on a white ground. Prayer rugs represent perhaps Turkey's greatest contribution to rug making, and examples dating from the 16th and 17th centuries are still in existence, although it is believed that the tradition is far older.

The motifs depicted on Muslim prayer rugs are the same no matter what their country of origin. They include representations of lamps, ewers and combs as well as, woven into the field and borders, verses from the Koran. Ushak prayer rugs made during the 17th century often include also star medallions and scattered floral motifs.

India

There is virtually no documentation of Indian carpet making prior to the 16th century, although it is known that, as in Persia, the art was supported by rulers and those in authority, and that workshops for carpet makers were established by these potentates. Even as late as the 17th century, India was – perhaps surprisingly – still importing Persian rugs in large quantities, and the country's Moghul rugs all too evidently owe a great deal to Persian design. Virtually all the surviving Indian rugs from this era depict formal floral designs, although there are a few from the early 17th century showing images of animals. These Indian pieces were unlike their Persian equivalents both in the species of animals depicted and in the fact that the depictions were realistic and asymmetric in style, rather than formal and geometric. Moreover, Indian rug makers favoured pictorial designs: any human and animal figures dominated the field rather than disappearing into the general pattern, as was almost always the case in Persian rugs. Nevertheless, although many elements of the Moghul floral rugs are characteristically Indian, the Persian influence is very clear. It seems possible that there was a considerable amount of interaction and exchange of ideas between Indian and Persian designers.

Moghul floral rugs can be categorized into several different groups. One consists of a lattice pattern with single flowers enclosed

in a white trellis frame; more commonly, however, the same theme was expressed in the form of single flowers enclosed within an abstract lattice, the flowers being in pink, white, yellow and/or green and portrayed on a red background. Another group, generally associated with Lahore, has rows of complete flowering shrubs, all pointing in the same direction, done on a red ground. This red ground is typical of Indian rugs; another common characteristic, especially among the smaller pieces, is an extremely finely knotted pile.

The Caucasus

Caucasian rugs originate from the area situated between the Black and the Caspian seas, a region now split between the Soviet Union and Iran. Until the conquest of this region by Russia during the 18th century it was constantly under attack by Arabs, Tartars, Mongols, Persians and others; consequently it became something of a cultural melting pot. Christianity and Islam fought for supremacy, a conflict reflected in the rug designs of the area.

The earliest known Caucasian rugs are called dragon rugs, and there is controversy over their date: some people believe they began to be made at the end of the 16th century while others reckon they date from the 15th century or earlier. Whatever the truth, these rugs display both Turkish and Persian influences. Characteristic of them are richness of colour and density of design, the colours and patterns becoming less intense and less detailed the later their date. Dragons, unicorns and other beasts, both fabulous and genuine, figure among diamond- or lozenge-shaped lattices; by the 18th century the designs had become so stylized that they verged on the geometric.

A southern Caucasian carpet of the early 19th century. The motif of the central panel is altered in each square to produce an irregular repeat. This gives the design a strong sense of movement.

17

At the same time as the dragon rugs were being produced, floral designs were being woven. One category of floral designs used interpretations of the Persian "vase" carpets while another – the floral lozenge type – was strongly influenced by contemporary Chinese design. Examples of this latter style exist from the 17th century right through to the 19th.

A third style was the floral shield, in which rows of individual flowers were depicted in an abstract form so that they resembled shields. All-over patterns of small floral sprays, resembling heraldic symbols, were also very popular; they were usually woven in red, yellow and blue on a white background.

Most early Caucasian rugs are of tribal origin, and it is difficult, solely through analysis of their design and colours, to determine exactly where they were made. However, the length of their pile and the type of wool used in their production can help to indicate the precise region where they were created.

Prayer rugs were widely produced in the Caucasus. They differ from the rugs made by other Muslim peoples in that there is, apparently, no qualm about including human and animal figures in the design. Both the field and the border patterns are very similar to those found on everyday rugs, being differentiated only by the inclusion of the typically Caucasian mihrab arch at the top of the field.

The Turkomans

Most Turkoman rugs originated in the Soviet states of Turkmenistan, Karakalpakstan and Uzbekistan, areas whose cultural heritage has been largely influenced by the Turkish and Mongol cultures. There are very few ancient rugs from this area still in existence, probably because they were seen at the time as functional objects rather than as artforms to be treasured. At present no known Turkoman rug can be dated with any degree of certainty to before 1800. These rugs show features common to many early rugs from other lands – including Caucasian, Ottoman and Seljuk designs. Two main features prevalent in Turkoman rugs are the colour-scheme – usually red, red-brown and red-blue – and the main decorative design element, the gul, an octagonal shape containing various different motifs.

East Turkestan

East Turkestan is a vast region spanning 1500km/1000 miles, from the city of Samarkand in the west to Khotan in the east. During its history East Turkestan has received cultural influences from many sources – Turkey, Persia, India, Mongolia and, finally, China. It is known through archaeological discoveries that floral and geometric patterns were established design themes by the 2nd or 3rd century AD.

The first hard evidence of rug making in China dates from the 14th century, although there is evidence to suggest that by the 12th century the art was a sophisticated one in Mongolia. Only in recent years have rugs made in East Turkestan been well received in Europe and the United States, and even today they command much lower prices than their Persian and Turkoman equivalents.

Perhaps the most characteristic design in the rugs of East Turkestan is the all-over pomegranate pattern; this was woven principally in Yarkand and Khotan. The design is thought to be one of the oldest deriving from the area, a representation of it having been found on a carved-wood ceiling dating back to around AD300.

Most of the East Turkestan rugs were made using wool, although a few surviving rugs were made entirely in silk. The pomegranate rugs generally have one of three border designs: a series of three-blossomed flower sprays; a series of zigzag lines (the Yun-Tsai-T'uo pattern) stylizing the Chinese wave pattern; and the "running-T" border, which again derives from Chinese weavings.

Rugs and carpets with a floral and lattice pattern continued to be popular throughout the 19th century. The lattices in these designs were sometimes very geometric in style, with interlocking star and diamond motifs.

China

China is not highly regarded for its wool production, but it has produced silk in vast quantities for the best part of 4000 years; the earliest Chinese weavings were done in silk. The Chinese tended to regard wool as a "barbarian" fibre, and most of the woollen items they possessed were of Mongolian origin. Chinese pile-knotted rugs – whether of silk or of wool – are a comparatively recent phenomenon.

Chinese carpets are the most distinctive in style of all Oriental rugs, possibly because Islam is not and never has been prevalent in China. Many pieces dating from the 7th–10th centuries depict flowers, birds, animals and human beings in colours such as brown, reddish-brown and blue on a white background. Others have large flowers set among flowing leaves and tendrils, or show scattered designs of clouds, pilgrims, plants growing from hillocks, etc. Although these early designs appeared on felted rugs, almost identical patterns were used on pile rugs made about 1000 years later.

Pile rugs were in use in China during the 13th century but these were probably of Mongol origin. In 1262 a factory was established in the Karakoram to supply the Imperial Chinese court with rugs and carpets. When the Mongols conquered China in 1272 a new approach to Chinese carpet design emerged, the Mongolian influence being very evident.

Very few Chinese motifs were purely decorative. Every symbol had its own particular meaning. Animals figured often on Chinese rugs; they included bats, butterflies, stags, fishes, unicorns, phoenixes, storks, cranes and geese, as well as the ubiquitous dragons. Flowers and fruits likewise figured widely.

The Chinese style remained remarkably unchanged even during the 18th and 19th centuries.

Europe

No one knows the precise origins of carpet making and rug making in Europe, although it is evident that Oriental carpets were imported at an early date; pile knotting would therefore have been known to the Europeans at this time, if not actually practised by them.

Carpets and rugs were virtually unknown in England until the 17th century. Before then the floor covering was generally of rushes or hay. When Eleanor of Castile married Edward I of England she brought many Spanish rugs with her, and carpets were much depicted in paintings of that time; however, it is believed that most of them were of Oriental origin. During the early Middle Ages rugs and carpets were considered to be treasures; as such they were far too precious to be put on the floor. They were probably used at first as table or altar cloths; by 1600 people were making a distinction between "table carpets" and "floor carpets".

Spain was probably the first European country to make pile rugs. The oldest known document to mention rug making dates from the 12th century. It states that rug making was already well established in Spain, and Spanish rugs were being exported to Egypt and the Near East. The Moorish conquest of Spain in the 8th century was largely responsible for the introduction of carpet making; it is recorded that Moorish palaces in Córdoba, Andalusia, contained some of the world's finest carpets.

The capital city of the Muslim dynasty of the Nasrids was Granada, and the insignia of the city, the pomegranate, was often included in the city's designs. The time of the Moorish occupation was the most fruitful period for Spanish carpet making although, as Christianity regained dominance, the Moors assimilated European decorative motifs into their work and combined them successfully with their traditional Muslim designs.

Spain

The use of heraldic arms and motifs has assisted greatly in the dating and identification of Spanish rugs. We know that Pope John XXII (1249–1334) ordered rugs made in Spain by the Moors for his palace at Avignon. Most of the heraldic carpets still existing from this period were made by Moors for Christians and utilized elements of both European and Islamic design. The field was usually decorated according to the Muslim tradition, with small polygon shapes, incorporating also star or cross motifs and sometimes representations of birds, animals or humans. Before the discovery of the Americas the predominant colours used were red and dark blue, along with small amounts of green, yellow and light blue. The opening up of trade with the New World resulted in the importing of dyes unknown in the Old, and from this time onwards the use of colour in the rugs was greatly enriched, with new varieties of red being brought from Mexico.

The greatest change in design direction came about as a result of the Moors leaving Spain, taking with them the Islamic secrets of dyeing and fixing. It was not generally a change for the better — indeed, it is fair to say that there was an overall deterioration in Spanish rugs. The process was a slow one, spread over centuries, but during the 16th and 17th centuries in particular there was a great reduction in the number of dyes used. Eventually a two-colour scheme became the consciously selected norm as Spanish rug makers gradually began to adopt patterns more in accordance with those of other European countries. By the 18th century the Islamic tradition had, with a few minor exceptions, died out altogether.

A local, rather cruder craft of rug making had developed in Granada, largely influenced by Moorish domination of the area. Dating the earliest of these is uncertain, but it is thought that they come from the late 15th century or early 16th. They were of a coarse weave with uncut loops, and many were fringed on all four sides. The designs were very simple, two-colour combinations being favoured — although some makers used up to ten colours. After the expulsion of the last of the Muslims, in 1609, many rugs incorporated religious symbols, initials, names and dates, but the peasant weavers were generally faithful to the old Moorish patterns, a tradition which continued into the 19th century.

Earlier, one effect of Spain coming under Christian rule had been that tapestries and other woven goods started to be imported from France, Venice and the Netherlands, and these became a dominant influence on the Spanish. One particularly popular pattern for early Spanish rugs came to be known as the Large Holbein because it made frequent appearances in the works of European artists. It had rows of octagons enclosed in squares with geometric patterning; the borders were often decorated in a stylized floral motif of Anatolian origin known in Spain as "the scorpion".

A large number of such rugs and carpets were woven at Alcaraz. It was during the 15th century that Western elements, influenced by the Gothic style of architecture prevalent in Europe at the time, began creeping into the designs of carpets made here. One of the motifs adopted was our old friend the pomegranate, which was popular in Granada and also in Italy.

Eastern Europe

Carpet making was developing also in Eastern European countries such as Poland and Romania. The influences on Polish rug designs were Russian and Islamic art; during the 16th century Poland was an important buyer of Turkish and Persian carpets. Polish carpets of that time were mostly in a flat weave and were made largely of silk, with gold thread incorporated.

During the 17th century there was a move to turn attention more towards Western designs, and carpet makers were brought in from Flanders to weave silk and wool in the Italian style. However, the idea did not catch on, and Polish carpet makers reverted to their traditional influences. Nevertheless, they began to develop their own style, using mainly blues and greens in naturalistic floral patterns.

Further south, in Romania, early rugs had designs that were mainly geometric. Later, depictions of animals and human figures were introduced, as were borders. Three distinct styles of Romanian rugs emerged. The area of Oltenian, in the south, produced carpets showing figures and hunting scenes, often on a black or green ground, and reminiscent of Persian miniatures. In contrast, carpets made in the northern region of Moldavia were usually of geometric design, with the "tree of life" symbol often being used. The colours in the Moldavian rugs were more subdued than in the Oltenian designs. Rugs from the central region, Transylvania, showed the greatest Oriental influence: they used designs of small, stylized flowers and sometimes incorporated birds and other animals.

Scandinavia

Perhaps surprisingly, the Eastern influence was prevalent also in Scandinavia. It is known that Oriental rugs had reached the Baltic area by the 15th century, at which time Norwegian and Swedish rugs were fairly rough, although a finer style was developed in Finland.

The first records of native Swedish rugs date from the middle of the 15th century. As with other Scandinavian rugs, they were important for trading purposes. They were often given as part-payment of a dowry, in which case they would be used as a cover for the marriage bed, having first served as the wedding rug on which the couple stood during the ceremony. During the 17th century the practice of using rugs as bedcovers declined, and designs started to incorporate pictorial elements – often, in the case of Norwegian rugs, religious motifs.

France

French rug making was apparently already established by the time of the Crusades, although no known pieces of that age survive today. It was not until the 17th century that the process really took root. Soon France was the European centre of carpet making.

In 1608 a former illuminator, Pierre Dupont, obtained a licence to make carpets in a workshop in the Louvre. In 1627 he took on a partner, Simon Lourdet, and, while retaining his premises in the Louvre, set up workshops in a piece of crown property, a one-time soap factory called the Savonnerie. Here he undertook to train orphans from the Hôpital de Bon Port in the art of rug making. The relationship between the two partners deteriorated, and some of the apprentices, taking advantage of this, left for England to set up rival factories, from which they began exporting goods to France.

The carpets made in both the Louvre and the Savonnerie workshops were of top quality. On Pierre Dupont's death the business was continued by his son Louis. By the middle of the 17th century the last vestiges of Eastern influence had disappeared, and the designs were completely European in style.

The Gobelins workshops, just outside Paris, were opened in 1662. A few years later, in 1667, they started manufacturing carpets for royalty, thereby paving the way for the development of a new French style. In the same year, both the Gobelins and the Savonnerie workshops were put under the direction of the court painter, Charles Lebrun. (It became standard in France to have a painter controlling the designs of the carpets, and this practice continued throughout the 18th century.) For the next 20 years or so these workshops were kept busy with commissions for Louis XIV, and they were to continue to flourish until the French Revolution. The Savonnerie workshops in particular suffered a reverse at this time since their carpet designs incorporated the royal insignia, and by 1805, although a few commissions were still coming in, only 19 people were employed there.

Before this change in the workshops' fortunes, Pierre Josse Perrot and a former pupil of his called Chevillon had, from 1760 onwards, introduced floral elements and rococo devices into the designs. Motifs included palm trees, shells, fleurs-de-lys and bat wings, the latter taking over from the baroque scrolls previously used. The colours became less intense: pink, yellow, pale blue and white were preferred as ground colours to black and brown.

During the First Empire a new style evolved as new designs were commissioned for the palaces. The decoration contained martial symbols, such as swords and shields. Simultaneously, there was also a movement towards carpets that were rather less grandiosely decorated, showing roses and marguerites in bold colours on a pale background. These designs were often influenced by those for formal gardens.

It should not be thought that the Savonnerie and Gobelins workshops were the only ones of importance in France. At the same time as the Savonnerie was being established another significant manufactory was in operation under private ownership. This was in Aubusson, an area long known for its carpet making. The carpets from Aubusson used much simpler designs than those from the Savonnerie – and were correspondingly much cheaper. These rugs and carpets were mostly purchased by the growing bourgeoisie, rather than by royalty and the nobility, although Louis XV did order two carpets from Aubusson in 1748. From the end of the 18th century the Aubusson designs tended towards a more linear appearance in response to the contemporary fashion for the Graeco-Roman style.

From 1800 an entrepreneur from Aubusson, Sallandrouze de la Mornaix, had a store in Paris selling Aubusson carpets. The following year he opened his own workshops to make thick-pile carpets, using workers poached from the Savonnerie. Soon he was one of the most important suppliers of carpets for the Emperor Napoleon. By 1810, however, times were hard for traditional carpet makers, because the invention in England of the power loom greatly decreased demand

A hand-knotted woollen pile carpet made in Exeter, England, about 1757 and clearly influenced by the French baroque/rococo designs emanating from the Jacquard factory at the time.

for the much more expensive hand-made pieces. Sallandrouze dismissed all of his workers in Paris and half of those in Aubusson. After 1830, in an attempt to compete with the style of carpets being produced in England, the company brought over to France carpet makers from Kidderminster, England. The carpet makers from England were to show the Aubusson workers how to set up and operate looms in order to make English-style moquette carpets. Unfortunately this operation was not particularly successful, and by 1871 things had deteriorated to such an extent that the company was declared bankrupt.

By this time the French had purchased the town of Pandicherri in India, where carpets made in French designs could be produced much more cheaply than in France herself. This continued into the 19th century, making it difficult for native French carpet makers to compete.

England

The influence of the Savonnerie reached England during the 18th century although, in the late 17th century, there had been an influx of Huguenot workers fleeing religious persecution in France.

The Axminster Carpet Factory was founded by Thomas Whitty, previously a manufacturer of woollen cloths, who was inspired to move to carpet making when he first came across Turkish carpets, some of which had been imported by an acquaintance of his in 1754. He went to a French-run factory in Fulham, near London, to see the process of carpet canufacture at first hand, and then returned to Axminster where his company began work on its first carpet in 1755. Most of the people he employed to work on his carpet looms were women and children – in part because their hands were smaller and hence perhaps nimbler but largely because their wages were lower than would have been those of a man. Before this very few women had been employed in Europe as weavers.

By the late 18th century, English carpet making was a flourishing industry. It was at about this time that it became established in Kidderminster, a town which had been a weaving centre for over 200 years; by 1800 carpet making was the foremost means of employment in the town. Kidderminster was rivalled by the Earl of Pembroke's carpet manufactory in Wilton, Wiltshire.

By this time the market was dominated by carpets of English manufacture since their style accorded much more than those of imported Oriental pieces with the architecture and furniture of the age. It had become fashionable to have a carpet whose pattern reflected the decoration of the painted ceiling. This was yet another reason to opt for an English-style carpet – since, while carpets could be imported, ceilings, generally speaking, could not.

Many of the prime English carpet makers of the day did not survive, but Whitty's Axminster factory kept on going from strength to strength. He himself was a keen amateur botanist, and his early carpets were characterized by their floral designs as much as by their use of colour. After 1800 classical motifs took precedence over floral ones. In 1828, however, the Axminster factory was destroyed by fire. Although new buildings were erected on the site, the company never recovered from the loss of both orders and skilled workers during the interim. In 1835 Samuel Whitty, who had inherited the company, was declared bankrupt, and in 1836 a man called Blackmore bought up the entire business, including all the machinery as well as a few weavers, and moved the operation to Wilton.

Despite growing competition, Blackmore was able to rebuild the Axminster business. Between 1836 and 1860 he increased the number of employees from 30–40 to more than 200. By the middle of the century the company had been commissioned to weave five carpets for Queen Victoria. The designs produced by the company were typical of the mixture of styles preferred in that period, incorporating Renaissance, Louis XIV, Italian and Persian elements.

In 1860 Blackmore sold the business to a London carpet maker, Alfred Lapworth. Lapworth died in 1871, and the company was then sold to Yates & Wills (later Yates & Co.). The factory flourished for a further 30 years. Yates opened a branch in the United States, and in England expanded his premises to include additional workshops in Southampton and Bemerton. All of these failed to survive because of his personal habits. Although he had been considered a pious man in Wilton, it transpired that he had been spending much of the company's money on gambling, drink and women in London and Chicago.

In 1905 the company was once more liquidated, but public funds were used to restore it, largely in order to maintain employment in the area. However, it continued to decline. Whereas in 1946 it possessed 102 looms, by 1956 only six hand looms remained. In 1957 it became the final hand-carpet factory in Britain to close its doors.

Hand weaving was no longer commercially viable – indeed, if truth be told, it had not been for some while. The development of carpet making during the 19th century had been due largely to the innovations in machinery stemming from the Industrial Revolution. By 1825 the French Jacquard mechanism had begun to replace the traditional hand loom. However, although automated manufacture was the key to greater turnover and hence greater profit, capital investment was required in order to bring in the new technology. This most of the smaller firms simply could not afford, and they went to the wall. For example, only two of the companies thriving in Kidderminster at the start of the 19th century are still in existence today.

So much for manufacture – what about English carpet design?

The Great Exhibition of 1851 brought about a discussion of the principles of design – although it had been acutely obvious since the 1830s that English design simply was not matching up to its European counterparts. At the Great Exhibition there was considerable criticism of the designs that had been submitted, particularly in terms of the adaptation of different styles and the overuse of naturalistic motifs – i.e., the abundant roses, ferns, wreaths, bouquets and scrolls – which frequently gave carpet designs a three-dimensional effect. After the Great Exhibition there was a move towards totally "flat" design, and Persian carpets regained popularity.

Undoubtedly the greatest Victorian pattern designer was William Morris. In 1878 he turned his attention from dyeing to weaving – a change heralded by his installation of a tapestry loom in his bedroom! Slightly earlier, he had begun to make designs for machine-woven carpets, between 1876 and 1883 producing 24 of these for the Wilton Royal Carpet Factory. Before he felt ready to undertake the work himself, however, he made an extensive study of Persian carpets, and the Persian influence is evident in all his rug designs. Morris's first pile carpets were woven in an attic in Queen's Square, London. Soon he moved production to Hammersmith and subsequently to Merton Abbey.

Once Morris had shown the way, other designers began to become interested in carpets. Many if not most of the great names of the Arts and Crafts movement and the Art Nouveau movement produced carpet designs. Although small Oriental-style designs were still prevalent, Art Nouveau certainly made an impact on rug design. At the same time there was also a general Jacobean revival, and this meant that genuine Oriental carpets increased in popularity.

North America

Before 1800 the floors of most North American homes were left uncovered, and it was not until the 1830s that significant amounts of domestically produced carpet-lay became evident. Motifs predominant among the 19th-century yarn-sewn rugs included patriotic symbols, people, ships, houses and animals — in marked contrast to the English practice of using designs made up of floral and geometric motifs.

North America gave birth to the hooked rug, probably in the late 1840s. The making of hooked rugs developed into a cottage industry in the far northern regions, where winter conditions hampered farming and fishing. By the end of the century these rugs were made throughout North America, although the technique was still regarded somewhat patronizingly as a "rustic craft", and the rugs were not favoured in fashionable homes.

However, since the earliest days, indigenous North American rug making has been dominated by the art of the Navajo Indians. At first the Navajos wove articles solely for personal use, but they were quick to recognize the demand for their wares from white traders.

Whereas traditional Navajo design had been abstract, by the 1890s the craftsmen were beginning to weave pictorial rugs. These were often highly elaborate, and frequently featured such images as animals, houses, railroads, American patriotic symbols and the Navajo supernatural beings known as "yeis". The meanings behind most Navajo symbols, though, are unknown today — even among the Indians themselves.

The most northerly of the Navajo weaving regions is Teec Nos Pos, which has a tradition of rug weaving dating back to the early 19th century. The Teec Nos Pos style is very similar to Middle Eastern designs, and it may be that the weavers were inspired by pictures of Persian rugs shown to them by traders.

The area known as Two Gray Hills is situated just to the east of the Chuska Mountains. Rugs made here are among the most tightly woven of Navajo products. Before 1915–20 the naturally coloured rugs were coarse, but then the quality began rapidly to improve, partly as a result of the inspiration and instruction of two traders,

George Bloomfield and Ed Davies. Commercial yarn and aniline dyes were discouraged, and the weavers were exhorted to stick to handspun wool. The predominant colours used in rugs from this area are white, black, tan and grey. The designs themselves are complex, usually consisting of a black border with an elaborate central panel of stepped diamond motifs, frets and zigzags. The swastika was often used until the late 1930s, when it virtually disappeared from the carpets because of its Nazi connotations.

The trader J. B. Moore was a resident of Crystal, New Mexico, from 1897 to 1911, and he introduced production line techniques into his rug business. His wife dyed the yarns herself using high-quality aniline dyes; the yarns were given only to the best weavers. Moore selected the designs, which often employed Oriental motifs: central diamonds were placed against light-coloured grounds, and there were strong, complex borders. He is thought to have been the first trader to produce a mail-order catalogue of Navajo rugs.

The tradition which he had started survived Moore's departure from the area, but during the 1930s and 1940s a completely different style of rug evolved here. These later designs were less complicated and were rendered using vegetable dyes in shades of brown, orange and yellow.

The earliest known example of a Navajo picture rug dates back to the late 1850s, but the tradition did not really start to flourish until the end of the century. It is still prevalent today among the Navajos. The rugs usually depict everyday scenes. The various motifs include the US flag, houses, animals, birds, Disney characters and graphic designs such as trademarks and advertising material. The designs have changed with the times so that, for example, where a train might have appeared in an early rug a more modern one might feature an aeroplane.

The 20th Century

The story of 20th-century rug making really starts in Finland. At the turn of the century the designer Akseli Gallan involved himself in the revival of the native arts of his country, and thereby initiated a new romantic current in Finnish design. Now, and again in the 1920s, traditional folk-art rug patterns were fashionable. This popularity declined during the 1930s, when the trend, as in the rest of Europe, came to be towards Cubism and functionalism. During the next decade attention shifted towards the toned rug, the outlines of whose patterns merged softly into each other. After 1950 the number of Finnish rug designers greatly increased. Most of these designers were women who had been tempted by competitions run by textile firms. Many modern rugs were produced which used longer tufts of yarn in an attempt to reflect the snow and ice of the northern landscape. The emphasis was on texture rather than on straightforward pattern.

In Germany, earlier in the century, the architectural style of the Bauhaus movement under the leadership of Walter Gropius had inspired all forms of the decorative arts. Gropius first made his aims known in Weimar in 1919; he had been influenced by the Deutscher Werkbund, which had been founded in 1907. One main idea of the Bauhaus movement was that artists and craftspeople should receive training through a form of craft appenticeship, but that their designs should make use of machine technology and thereby satisfy the requirements of mass production. The first Bauhaus *Lehrmeister* to work in weaving was Hélène Börner, who had once worked with Henri Van de Velde, founder of the Deutscher Werkbund. In 1920 the painter Georg Muche was appointed *Formmeister*. Many designs were done for Börner and Muche by Paul Klee.

When the Bauhaus was relocated to Dessau in 1925 there was a split between Muche and Gunta Stölzl. In Dessau the emphasis was placed on mechanical weaving and dyeing, and Muche favoured the idea that machine weaving should be exploited to the full. Stölzl, by contrast, was not satisfied that the machines were ready to adopt the advances that she and her students had made on the hand looms. She demanded that there should be freedom for hand weavers to keep developing new ideas. In 1926 Muche left the Bauhaus and Stölzl took his place. Her practical approach meant that experimentation continued in the workshops. Many of the ideas hatched there were subsequently used successfully by German manufacturers – a consideration that did not stop the Nazis from closing down the Bauhaus in 1933.

The Bauhaus movement exerted an influence in countries outside Germany, in some more than in others. In France, for example, while Bauhaus ideas certainly had an effect, carpet designers were more influenced by the works of the Cubist painters. Several Modernist rugs were shown at the Paris Exhibition of 1925. These pieces were revolutionary in that they dispensed with a border, thereby leaving more space for an outward movement of line and shape. The choice of a white or off-white ground was also to be of extreme importance.

At this time design in Britain was being widely criticized on the grounds that it tended to imitate rather than innovate – even though fashion had turned towards a new style of interior design in which the emphasis was on the use of light and space, and in which paintings were losing their popularity in favour of designed rugs. The Cubist movement in art inspired an abstract style which was functional rather than purely decorative, and which was in direct contrast to the by then unfashionable excesses of Victorian design.

The first major force in 20th-century British carpet design in fact came in the form of two North Americans, the Vorticist poster designer E. McKnight Kauffer and the textile designer Marian Dorn; it is probable that Dorn was responsible for first drawing Kauffer's interest to rug design. The major carpet manufacturers were, in general, reluctant to risk producing such avant-garde designs, so most of these rugs were made either by small companies or by Kauffer himself. Many of the rug designers involved were also graphic artists, selling their rugs as one-off items. All of these rugs were, for obvious reasons, very expensive.

The economic slump of the 1930s meant that expensive luxury items such as designed rugs were suddenly less than buoyant in the marketplace. The reaction was led by the firm of Morton Sundour, which began producing Modernist rugs created by the Edinburgh Weavers, itself a company run by Alastair Morton. The Edinburgh Weavers attempted to produce rugs which accorded with current aesthetic trends and to bring weaving into line with architecture, as advocated by the Bauhaus. Hans Aufseeser met Morton in Düsseldorf in 1932 and approved of his ideas; subsequently Aufseeser did many designs for Morton's enterprise. Morton opened showrooms in Hanover Square and Bond Street, London; on sale were carpets and fabrics designed by Dorn, Kauffer, Aufseeser, Marion Pepler, Ashley Havinden, Terence Prentis and Paul Nash.

This design movement barely survived the war years. Dorn and Kauffer returned to their native United States, and most of the rest of the designers in due course turned their attentions to other fields. During the 1950s the fashion in British rugs changed to favour the Scandinavian idea that texture was more important than straightforward visual design. Despite the fact that their creative impetus of the 1930s was a thing of the past in more than one sense, the Edinburgh Weavers continued to thrive. Royal Wilton, who had supported the trend, stopped hand-loom production in 1957.

The innovativeness of the pre-war years has yet to be replaced by any individual new movement, although there has been a revived interest in Oriental rugs – a fact mirrored by their rise in value. Recently, however, modern designers have begun to turn their attention once more to rugs and carpets. It is to be hoped that, in times to come, these designers will be looked back upon as having been among the historical "greats".

Although this brief survey has taken us to many parts of the world, it cannot hope to be complete. However, it is clear that rug making is today a focus of activity in most countries of the world and that some of the designs currently being produced are visually and texturally very exciting. For the evidence to support this statement the reader need go no further than the pages of this book ... although, of course, we hope that you will go *much* further!

2

DESIGN
CONSIDERATIONS

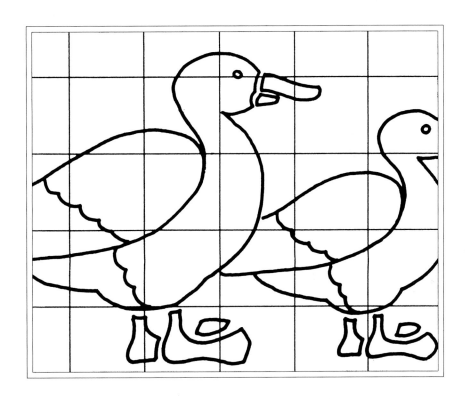

Whatever the ability of a rug maker, the design of the rug itself is obviously a matter — if not *the* matter — of fundamental importance. Good rug makers almost always spend considerable time at the planning stage before they start any of the manual labour. It is often forgotten that people commissioning rugs should likewise spend some while thinking about the design they want, because otherwise they will be dissatisfied with the final product and will have only themselves to blame.

The overall aim must be to achieve a balance between all the design elements: to choose a simple example, a wide selection of colours arrayed in complex motifs will be lost in a long-pile shaggy rug, but could be used effectively to compensate for a lack of textural interest in a rug with a very short pile.

The colour and pattern should obviously be chosen to suit both the rug maker's taste and the other elements of the decor into which the rug must fit. The texture of the finished rug must likewise be planned — indeed, texture is as important as any other part of the design if the resulting rug is to be a success. For example, a long-pile rug would offset to good effect a smooth surface, such as a polished wooden floor, whereas a short-pile rug would better complement a deeply textured carpet.

Similarly, if the existing flooring is highly patterned, then a fairly plain rug, perhaps picking up one of the colours in the carpet, will almost certainly be aesthetically more pleasing than a complex design, which is likely to clash. Rug designers must consider also the type of room in which the rug is to be used. They have to decide at the outset whether they want the design to complement or contrast with the existing decor. A very modern design in bold colours would probably be out of place in a traditionally furnished setting — but might look stunning in a neutral, sparsely furnished room. Mind you, harmonizing the rug with its setting does not mean that the rug's colours necessarily have to be identical with those in the curtains, nor that the design motif has to be an exact replica of one from the furniture coverings. Juxtaposed differences, however, should involve the art of "planned" contrast, not accidental clashes. Designs that quarrel with each other are the last thing you want in a room that is intended to exude an atmosphere of restfulness.

A splash of colour can be set down most dramatically and yet quite appropriately in a room which is otherwise decorated in black and white, and likewise a monochrome rug can look good in a very colourful room, but the choice must be obviously stated; i.e., some part of the design or texture of the rug must deliberately reflect, exaggerate or even flaunt one or more aspects of the rug's surroundings. Such a planned expression of individuality can create a humorous tone and is unlikely to upset the balance of the room — unless that is what you set out specifically to do. Contrasts, if carefully used, can provide scope for individualism while remaining within the bounds of other people's tastes and not proving impossible to live with.

Even rya and flossa rugs, which are characterized by their brilliant and vibrant colouring, can be used for effective contrast. These rugs are far from arbitrary in their design. Usually they have a simple theme which unifies the bold combination of several shades tied together using the same knot.

The choice of sources of inspiration for a rug design is limited only by the designer's imagination. Details from a painting or photograph can be adapted and enlarged to form the basis of the design, as can items encountered in everyday life. Most rug designers make a habit of being observant when they are out and about: even a mossy path or an old brick wall can disclose a surprisingly pleasing and subtle palette if really *looked at*. Everyone can try this for themselves. If you open your eyes to ordinary everyday objects – even industrial sites or urban landscapes – you can discover the variety of tones and shapes which go to make them up.

If total coordination is desired, the design of the rug can be based on the patterns in the existing decor – for example, in the curtains or the wallpaper. A motif or section of the design can be picked out and enlarged to form the focal point of the rug design, or used in the border of what is otherwise a plain rug.

Enlarging Your Design

The process of enlarging a design need not be difficult. The technique described below is, in fact, very simple, yet enables the designer to make a fairly accurate enlargement (or, for that matter, reduction) while at the same time maintaining the correct proportions. For these reasons it is probably the most common method used.

First a grid of equal squares is drawn onto the original (see diagrams, pages 34–5). Some people prefer not to draw directly onto the original, especially if it is in a book or some other treasured possession; this problem can be overcome by first tracing the outline of the design and drawing the grid onto the tracing. The size of the squares used depends, obviously, on the size and complexity of the original design; however, they should probably be between 3mm/$\frac{1}{8}$in and 25mm/1in to a side. A simple calculation is then used to find out how big each square should be in the final result: for example, if the end product is to be 20 times the size of the original, all the designer has to do is multiply the dimensions of each square by 20. The squares are then drawn accordingly onto a piece of paper the size that the rug is planned to be, and the contents of each square are sketched in. Finally this design, without the squares, is transferred onto the base fabric of the planned rug.

Colour, Size, Pattern and Texture

Shape and size are obviously important factors when a designer is considering the context in which a rug will appear, but they are certainly not the only ones. The choice of colour, pattern and texture should take account of such considerations as

- the amount of light falling on the floor
- the other shapes, designs and textures within the setting
- the amount of wear and tear to which the rug will be subjected
- last but not least, the effect that different colours and patterns within the rug will have on its overall look

As we have seen, the choice of design should be relevant to the particular spot in which the rug is to be placed. Today's rugs are so diverse in style, colour and texture that they can be the most individual expression of personal taste. Unfortunately, the limitations imposed by the shapes and colours of the existing features in a room have to be recognized if the design that looks so good hanging on a plain-white gallery wall is going to live in harmony when set alongside your favourite marble flooring or your rococo-style chaise longue.

It's easy enough to enlarge your original design. Simply draw a grid of squares over it and then increase the size of those squares until you get the right proportions for the final rug. Draw into each square the relevant shapes. Obviously you can use the same technique to reduce a design.

The size of a rug is in some ways as difficult to decide as its design. It is unlikely that anyone will make or commission a rug that is eye-offendingly too large, but it is a simply made mistake to choose something that, in the event, turns out to be too small. The rug that makes itself at home in the smaller dining room will almost certainly look like nothing more than a limp, forlorn rag in even the most modest of banqueting halls. Many rug designers will therefore cut out a paper pattern and put it in the position where the finished rug is intended to go. It makes sense to go a step further and lay down an idea of the proposed colour and texture – perhaps using fabric samples – before deciding whether or not the planned rug will be of the right size to sit easily in its environment.

Associated with the matter of correct size and shape is the basic choice of design motif – in other words, the sizes and shapes *within* the rug. An appreciation of the relationship that design and pattern have with the use of space is especially important when one is designing one's own rug; certainly it helps considerably if one is aware of how a mass of colour arranged in a tight space underfoot can look disastrously incongruous when placed against a spaciously set design that covers a much more expansive wall space. In a large open area it is important to avoid ineffectual design motifs and insignificant washes of colour, neither of which will add anything to a much grander surrounding. Similarly, a large bold design will often be overbearing in a confined space where the motifs used on the draperies and wallpapers are likely to be small but often repeated. In general, a smaller pattern repeated many times in a rug will not necessarily look out of place in a large room where the motifs used in the other elements of the decor are likewise large (so long as the rug is the right size for its environment), but, in a small room, any existing design motif must be scaled down if it is to work harmoniously with the rest of the furnishings.

Mixing the traditional with the contemporary can be dangerous, but the end product need not be aesthetically displeasing. As long as there is a unity of shape, design and colour, it is quite possible that a modernistically bold stretch of colour can add harmonious excitement to a room whose other furnishings are done in quieter tones and colouring. Conversely, a more earthy floor covering can "lift" a room that is otherwise abstract in its design.

Another thing that designers consider when planning their rugs is the matter of perspective. Rugs are usually looked down upon, and from many different angles. When you select a pattern it is a good idea if you consider that a single large image may be disturbing to the eye from any viewpoint other than that which you originally envisaged: a rug that looks great when hung on a wall can look dreadful when placed where it ought to be, on the floor.

Again, if a rug is to be set in a room with a clutter of chair-legs, lampstands, etc., a single image may become quite lost, even in the largest of rooms. The obvious solution is to scale down the design.

This is not just a question of straightforwardly reducing its size. Every aspect of colour, texture and pattern must be kept in balance — something which in certain cases can prove to be impossible. In a rag rug, for example, a large image that is perfectly clear may lose all definition if it is scaled down.

Bright colours are shown to full advantage in areas of fewer furnishings and wide open spaces. If they are contained within a bordering of darker colour, it is a good idea to consider the effect this will have when the rug is in its chosen setting. It might be that the border will visually blend in with the surrounding carpet, so that the remainder of the design seems to jump out at the viewer — in other words, that the rug will fail to "lie flat" on the floor. In general, unless specially sculpted for effect, a rug design should always remain "flat" on the ground as otherwise there will be parts of it which will be just dull expanses of colour lying miserably on the floor.

When considering this aspect of unified colours, it is helpful to put samples of each colour intended for the room alongside samples of each of the others and to take a good hard look at the effect. Colours can play strange and unexpected tricks when placed next to each other. Another thing to consider in this context is the matter of lighting. Colours will interplay in different ways with each other depending on the amount and nature of light in the room.

Wear, Materials and Techniques

When choosing the colours and textures of floor coverings, some consideration must be given to matters of wear and tear. The siting of the rug clearly plays a part. Barefoot traffic in the bedroom is something quite different from the trundling of hob-nailed boots in the hall!

As a very general rule, medium shades of colour and smaller, more repeated designs are better suited for areas which receive a considerable amount of wear. Too much light or pale colouring will show dirt quickly and possibly become permanently stained, while large expanses of dark colouring will allow dust, fluff and other particles to show up only too clearly.

The materials that make up a floor covering affect every process from the selection of colour and pattern to the decision about the rug's final home. From the rug designer's point of view, the choice of materials affects the choice of technique — and the same is obviously true the other way round. These, once decided, affect the choice of design. For example, a successful hand-tufted rug usually has a less detailed design because the texture and the process of making it do not permit perfect linear definition. However, hand tufting allows a very personal and precise choice of colour, because one can dye one's own materials, and this makes up for the lesser amount of detail possible in the pattern. If you are set on having a linear or geometric pattern you would be better to opt for a weaving technique. Tapestry weaving gives you greater control of design and intricate detail than loom weaving can.

As with colours, the determination of the materials to be used depends to a great extent on where the rug is to be placed. Coarser and tougher materials are more appropriate for well trodden, down-to-earth settings. Pure wool will not remain unsullied for long beside a fireplace that is in active use, for example, or by an outside door. Conversely, a heavy, coarse woven rug is almost certain to look a little, shall we say, inhospitable in a romantic bedroom. These are obviously extreme examples, but it should be emphasized that the texture of a rug – and hence the materials used in it – must be considered in terms not just of the rug itself but also of its final setting and use.

It might seem from this chapter that the process of designing a rug is a veritable maze, designed to trap the inexperienced or unwary. In fact, it is much less daunting than it can appear. All you have to remember to do is to think of the problem as a whole, rather than tackle the details one by one. If you can visualize from the start the coordinated combination of colour, design and texture as it will appear in the proposed setting, and the way in which each of them takes on character within the rug, then most of the design options select themselves.

3

RAG RUGS

The tradition of making rag rugs is a long one, dating from early times in Scandinavia. It is generally associated with·folk art and the hearthrug, both in Europe and in North America, where the technique has perhaps been more widely employed. While the practice of hooking short lengths of wool or cut-up rags through a hessian (burlap) or canvas base has changed little over the centuries, a contemporary design-oriented approach can confound our jaded perceptions of rag rugs as drab, homely objects. Instead, they can be things of beauty.

BASIC TECHNIQUES

Making rugs from rags is economical, since most of the basic materials are already either in your possession or available cheaply at jumble sales, in charity shops or anywhere else that sells discarded fabric. Any type of fabric can be used that does not fray easily, although woollen fabrics work particularly well because of wool's natural resistance to dirt. Fabric that has been stained, scorched or moth-eaten need not be discarded, because one can cut the offending areas away. Fabrics of different textures can be mixed in a single rug so long as they are all of a similar weight: wonderful effects can be created by mixing herringbones, tweeds and twills, and the use of such fabrics can result in a rug that not only looks attractive — because of the beautifully subtle, natural shades of the fabrics — but also disguises dirt and stains. Finally, there is no reason, aside from expense, why new fabrics cannot be used instead of rags, either in conjunction with scavenged fabrics or on their own.

Once the fabrics have been gathered, it is essential that they be thoroughly washed — not just for reasons of elementary hygiene but also because there is a chance that one of them may at some point have served as an egg-laying site for moths; besides, if the finished rug is itself to be washable the fabrics from which it is made should be "pre-shrunk" as much as possible. Woollens should be washed, too, because felting is positively desirable in this instance. Only after the fabrics have been washed can they be dyed — any commercial dye will do. It does not matter if the dyeing comes out patchy — indeed, any tonal variations will add interest to the finished rug.

Canvas is generally used as the backing fabric. It should not be too closely woven, as then it would be much harder to work on. The backing is prepared by cutting it to the right size, plus a hem of about 5cm/2in on all sides; the central lines, both horizontal and vertical, are marked on it. Also, if the rug is going to have an unusual shape, this should be marked onto the backing fabric (but not cut out until the work has been completed). The raw edges are usually finished either by stitching or using carpet binding, although there is a third method which can be used if the backing is a warp cloth, as employed in hooking. The edges can be finished by decorating them with fringing. Before the design is hooked, several threads are removed from the selvedge. A row of buttonhole stitch, working into each mesh and over three threads, is worked with a darning needle along the outline of the pattern, using the threads drawn from the backing fabric. This prevents the base fabric from unravelling and also substitutes for a hem. Once the hooking has been completed the warp fabric is cut along the short sides of the rug to about 7.5–10cm/3–4in from the buttonhole stitch and the cross threads are unravelled. The long edges are trimmed along the row of buttonhole stitching.

There are two basic methods of rag-rug making. Often these are called, respectively, hooking and prodding. A more modern technique of hooking is the punch-needle method. In this chapter we shall look at the basic techniques involved for each of these ways of making rugs. However, first we should consider the topic of rug frames – not just for rag rugs but in other areas of rug making.

The Rug Frame

Only rarely is it absolutely necessary to use a rug frame, especially in the making of hand-hooked and tapestry rugs; a notable exception is when working a punch-needle rug, as with this technique the base fabric must be kept taut. However, rug makers working in all styles often prefer to use a frame because they feel that it facilitates working and helps them to regulate the tension of the knots or stitches.

There are several types of frame available, and most of them are suitable for tapestry, hand-hooked and punch-needle rugs. Generally a rectangular shape is used; if the backing material is canvas this is actually essential, since circular or oval frames can cause the canvas to distort.

Some frames come with a stand; others are flat, so that they can be worked on a table or even on one's lap. The flat frames are much more portable and therefore more convenient for rug makers who want to carry the work around with them rather than have it set up in a single studio. Flat frames are also very much cheaper. However, frames with stands are a lot easier to work with as they leave both

A rug frame is used to prevent the foundation material distorting; it also leaves both your hands free to work the rug. 1 In the simplest way of using the frame, the base fabric is fastened to both of the side bars and you work on the area between them. 2 Usually, though, the bars can be moved, so that you can roll away completed areas of the work and expose new areas of backing fabric.

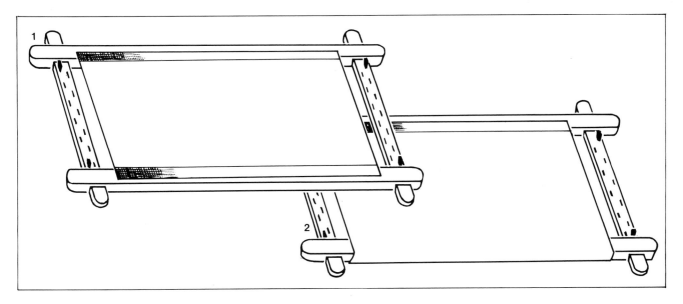

hands free and are adjustable to any angle, so that the rug maker can easily gain access to the underside of the work.

Alternatively, one can improvise a frame using four pieces of wood knocked together to form a rectangle. And there is no reason why, provided it is sturdy enough, an old picture frame cannot be used. Of course, these alternatives do not give the rug maker the facilities offered by the commercially made frames, but they do represent a considerable saving. All in all, with rug frames as with so much else, you pays your money and you takes your choice.

Most frames designed for rug making are fitted with movable bars at top and bottom so that, as each section of work is completed, it can be rolled away to expose a fresh area of backing fabric. Usually webbing is stapled to the roller bars so that the backing fabric can be simply tacked onto them. The base fabric must also be attached to the sides of the frame. This is not difficult to do: each time you start on a fresh area you can merely lace strong thread through the fabric and wind it around the side bars. Before you start work it is essential that you position the fabric in the frame so that the grain runs straight — otherwise all sorts of distortions can occur.

Prodding

The prodding method of making rag rugs is suitable only for simple designs that concentrate mainly on mixing colours and/or textures, such as parallel stripes or all-over mottling. Prodded rugs are much coarser than hooked rugs and have a thicker pile, and consequently they are much harder to keep clean.

They are made by pushing strips of rag through the backing fabric

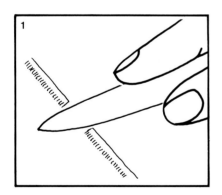
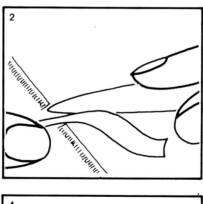
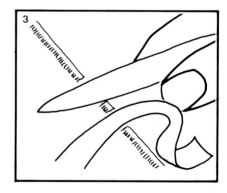
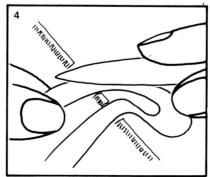
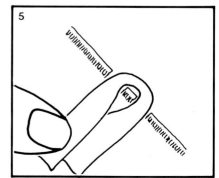

Prodding a rag rug. 1 Start with the wrong side facing you, and use the prodder (peg) to make a hole in the backing fabric. 2 Push one end of your strip of fabric through the hole. 3 Make another hole close to the first one, again using the prodder. 4 Prod the other part of the strip of fabric through the new hole. 5 Pull the strip of fabric tight and move on to the next pair of holes. If you want a tighter pile you can prod the first end of the next piece of fabric through one of these holes.

using a pointed implement, the prodder (or peg). When a frame is used the prodding is done from the wrong side; otherwise it is done from the right side. Different effects can be achieved by using strips of material of different sizes, and it is a good idea to experiment in this area before starting the work in order to discover the most pleasing effect. As a general guide, a shaggy pile will be produced using strips measuring about $10cm \times 4cm/4in \times 1\frac{1}{2}in$.

If a frame is being used the fabric is stretched across it and secured either as described above or simply with drawing pins or staples. The work is done from the back of the base fabric. First a hole is made in the fabric and then a strip of material is pushed nearly halfway through this using the prodder. Next a second hole is made, close to the first, and the other part of the strip is prodded through this. The work continues in rows until the rug is completed.

If the prodding is worked without a frame the backing fabric is folded, with the wrong sides together, and a hole is made with the prodder through the double thickness of fabric about $1cm/\frac{1}{2}in$ from the folded edge. The strip of rag is folded in half lengthwise and then prodded through the hole so that there are equal amounts of fabric on either side. This is carried on all the way along the row before the backing fabric is unfolded so that it lies flat. The next fold is made close to the first one – perhaps $3cm/1\frac{1}{4}in$ away – and the process is repeated. This is continued across the full extent of the backing material. Once the final fold has been flattened out and the edges have been finished, the main work of the rug has been completed.

All that remains to be done is the lining. It is not advisable to line a rag rug as small stones and other sharp objects can work their way down through the pile and become trapped between the lining and the backing fabric. As the rug is walked on over the months or years, these objects will wear a hole in the backing fabric.

The rug can be lined by covering the underside with a rubbery type adhesive which will both keep the loops in place and give the rug a non-slip undersurface. It is not absolutely essential to do this, but there are obvious long-term advantages. The adhesive should be applied over the entire underside of the rug, right up to the edging, and then smoothed down using the applicator supplied with the adhesive.

Hand-hooked Rugs

In hand hooking, long strips of fabric are hooked through a backing fabric using an implement that looks rather like a jumbo-sized crochet hook that has been mounted in a wooden handle (see diagram on page 52). As with other rag rugs, superb special effects can be created by shading small areas and motifs in lighter and darker tones of the same colour. The most commonly used backing fabric is burlap, although cotton and linen fabrics, known as warp cloths, are available as alternatives. The quantity of rag material needed to make a rug varies and will depend on the type of fabric used, but a general guideline is that 250g of material will be sufficient to cover about 1000cm² of backing fabric ($\frac{1}{2}$lb per square foot); most rug makers allow extra to be on the safe side.

The width of the cut strips depends on the type of fabric being used. The strips should be cut as narrowly as possible, according to the density of the weave of the fabric. Certainly strips cut from the same type of fabric should have uniform widths. The longer each strip is, the better.

Hooking is a very simple technique of rug making, although anyone who has never tried it before is advised to practise for a while before embarking on their first rug. The hook is held above the base material with one hand while the other holds a long strip of fabric beneath the base material. The hook is then pushed through the base and a loop of fabric is drawn through to the desired height of pile. The next loop is formed in exactly the same way and as close as possible to the first – although not so closely as to pucker the base material. The loops should all be of the same size, to ensure a uniformity of pile; the height of the pile is determined both by the type of fabric used and by the width of the strips. Rug makers wanting a firmer and harder-wearing pile – and who does not! – give the hook a slight twist just as they are pulling through each loop. The process is repeated until the strip of fabric runs out, at which point both of the loose ends are pulled through and trimmed to the same height as the rest of the pile.

When the rug maker is not using a frame, normal practice is for the motifs and design areas to be worked first, and to do as much of each colour at a time as possible. Once the motifs and design areas have been completed, the background can then be filled in. Rug makers who use a frame, however, complete one entire section, all of the motifs and the background, before rolling on to expose a fresh piece of base fabric.

Finally the completed rug is lined using a heavy-duty hessian (burlap) fabric, unless the backing canvas used is very strong.

The Punch-needle Method

A more modern technique is the punch-needle method, which is worked with yarn rather than with fabric strips. It has been in popular use for the last half-century or so. Its great advantage over traditional hand hooking is that the punch needle automatically produces loops of uniform length, so that the final rug has a soft, close pile. The needle is usually adjustable, so that the maker can select the precise height of loops which he or she desires, and it is supplied with a range of points suitable for different weights of yarn. For a backing you can use any strong coarsely woven fabric; just make sure that the weave is broad enough for the needle to pass through. If you're using hessian (burlap) as your backing, choose a heavy type.

The design is drawn on the wrong side of the base fabric, since this

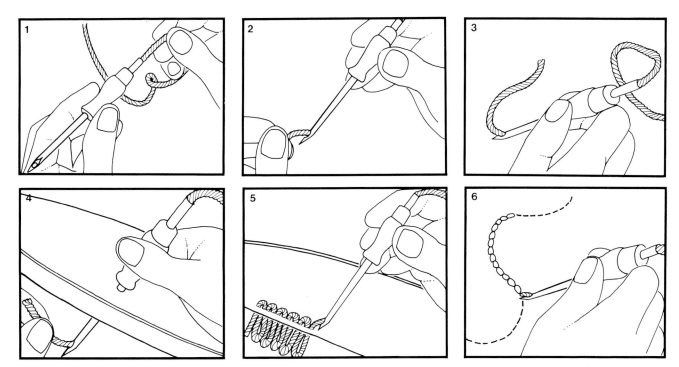

is the side from which the needle will be inserted; obviously, the design is reversed before being transferred to the base fabric. Once the finished edge has been determined, the fabric is stretched taut on a frame, wrong-side uppermost.

The hook of the needle contains an eye, and through this eye the yarn is threaded, according to the manufacturer's instructions. The threaded needle, held vertically, is pushed through the base fabric, so that the end of the yarn is drawn just through to the underside (i.e., the right side) of the work (see diagrams). The needle is next raised until its point is just above the top surface of the base fabric, and then drawn across to the place where the first loop is to be made; to make the loop, push the needle through the fabric as far as it will go. This process is continued until the section has been completed or the piece of yarn has been finished; the loose ends of yarn are trimmed as in a hooked rug (see page 44).

As you work you have to ensure that the yarn feeds freely across the back of your hand and through the needle so that a regular tension is maintained; otherwise the loops will be irregular – or perhaps will fail to be formed at all! When further rows are being worked the finished loops are held away from the current row in order to avoid tangling.

Using the punch needle. 1 Insert the end of the yarn into the base of the needle, and push it gently down the shaft. 2 When the end of the yarn appears, catch hold of it and thread it through the eye. Make sure that the yarn is moving through the needle easily. 3 Hold the needle in an upright position as you work, with its slotted side facing in the direction in which you wish to work. 4 Push the needle as far as it will go between the warp and weft threads. Catch hold of the end of yarn. Still holding the yarn, withdraw the needle. 5 Keeping hold of the loose end, slide the needle along a few threads and once more push it through the fabric as far as it will go. Again catch hold of the end of yarn and withdraw the needle, to form a loop. Repeat to create the effect you desire. 6 If you change the direction of your line of looping, remember to turn the needle so that its slotted side is always facing in the direction you are going. If you want to change colours, cut the yarn short and poke it through to the right side; then rethread the needle and start again.

GALLERY OF DESIGNERS

Sara Parnell

Oriental textiles, North American decorative arts and English needle-work are all among Sara Parnell's sources of visual inspiration

Above: This rag rug by Sara Parnell takes its inspiration from the type of rugs designed by the Navajo Indians. Its rich earthy tones are very much in keeping with the traditional colours used by the Navajos. *Right*: Sara Parnell has a great fondness for pressed and dried flowers, as we can see from this rag rug which she created.

although, they are not always immediately apparent in her work. Her enthusiasm for drawing pressed, dried and living flowers is more directly evident. The flowers in her rugs are often represented pictorially, in contrast with the textural representation of floral scenes which features in much of the work of Julia Burrowes (see below).

Sara finds that much of the fun in rug making is to be found in the dyeing process. She often spends several weeks at a time devoted to it, using chemical hot-water dyes on torn cotton rags.

Her particular long-term aim is to make her work progressively finer, so that she can make ever more use of detail. She is also planning to produce some much larger pieces.

Julia Burrowes in her studio, dyeing the fabrics for her rugs.

Below left: Julia Burrowes selecting colours for her rug. *Below right*: The partially completed rag rug. *Bottom left*: In this detail we can see how many tones and shades are used in Julia's rugs. *Bottom right*: Julia using a latch hook to prod the fabric through the canvas. *Opposite*: Rag rug by Julia Burrowes.

Julia Burrowes

One important source of Julia Burrowes's inspiration comes from her memories of her childhood in Yorkshire. She recalls seeing her first rag rugs in the homes of the grandparents of some of her school-friends. Often the houses were typical Yorkshire terraced back-to-backs, with the rugs being given pride of place on the stone-flagged kitchen floor. In a setting with a black-leaded kitchen range and expanses of dark wood, the rug, with its mass of textures and pattern, provided a cheerful focal point for the room. The patterns of these rugs were usually made up of diagonal stripes whose widths

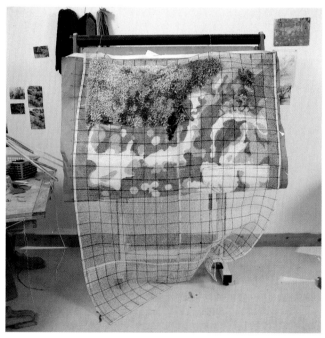

varied according to the amount of each material that was available.

The colours of those old rag rugs were almost always of necessity muted. Julia has far more freedom, and uses all the colours of the spectrum in order to maximize the visual impact of her works. The range of colours available to her is increased yet further by the fact that she dyes all her own wools – usually blanket-type fabrics that contain no synthetics – in a large vat in her studio. She uses the dyeing process much as she would create colours on her palette, mixing just the right tones and shades she requires for each rug. When she uses hot dyes they have the effect of changing not only the colour of the fabric but also its texture, giving it an almost felted feel which becomes more apparent in the soft, matted look of the finished rugs.

Her early rugs were based on abstract shapes which she treated in an impressionistic – almost pointillist – style, so that the overall pattern becomes more obvious the further away from the rug you get. She achieved this by using subtle gradations of tone and shade, fading in and out over the entire rug.

She has recently begun to develop this careful and painstaking technique into a more pictorial style. Her new designs, which allow her even greater scope for sweeps of colour, employ rather more organic shapes and floral motifs based on accurate observations in her own garden and the nearby woods. It is her attention to nuance and detail that marks Julia's rugs out as the objects of interest and harmony that they so patently are.

PROJECT

A HAND-HOOKED RAG RUG – ''TRADITIONAL CRAZY DESIGN WITH SCROLL BORDER''

This hand-hooked rug has been designed by Joy Scott. The materials used should be easy enough to acquire.

You will need
- a hook
- a frame to keep the backing fabric taut
- remnants of fabric – old clothes from jumble sales, plain woollens or tweeds, cottons, jersey or whatever is to hand
- for the backing fabric, jute hessian (burlap) with a weave open enough for the hooking tool to move easily through it

Method
This technique uses long strips of fabric to create a close loop pile. You can use a variety of sizes of loops to give different pile heights, although the instructions here assume that you are using strips of equal length.

Hem the fabric before you attach it to the frame. The hem should be turned towards the right side of the rug. Sew the fabric onto the frame by matching the centre points of the rug edge and the frame rail. Using strong thread, oversew the fabric to the webbing of the frame.

Use a light pencil to mark out the design onto the foundation fabric. Start to hook with the right side of the fabric facing up.

Start to hook by holding the strip of fabric in your left hand below the hessian (burlap), and work from right to left (assuming that you are right-handed). Face the hook in the direction of movement and push it down through the hessian (burlap) at a slight angle; bring the end of the strip up through to the top of the hessian (burlap). (See diagrams on page 52.)

Push the hook through the hessian (burlap) to the left and fairly close to the previous movement, and pull up the strip. (See diagrams on page 52.)

On top of the hessian (burlap) gently form a loop about 1cm/$\frac{1}{2}$in high. (See diagrams on page 52.)

Continue in this way, remembering to finish each strip by pulling the ends up to the top. Start a new strip in the same hole as ended the previous strip.

Designed by Joy Scott, "Traditional Crazy Design with Scroll Border" is a hand-hooked rag rug.

Joy Scott at work on this hand-hooked rag rug. She is working the rug on a frame in order to prevent distortion.

Hand-hooking a rag rug. 1 Work from the right side. Hold the strip of fabric below the canvas and push the hook down at a slight angle to catch the top of the loop. 2 Use the hook to pull the top of the loop back up through the backing material. 3 Push the hook through a hole in the canvas near to the first one and again catch hold of a loop. 4 Continue in this way, remembering to start and finish a strip by pulling the ends up to the top. Start a new strip in the same hole as the end of the previous strip.

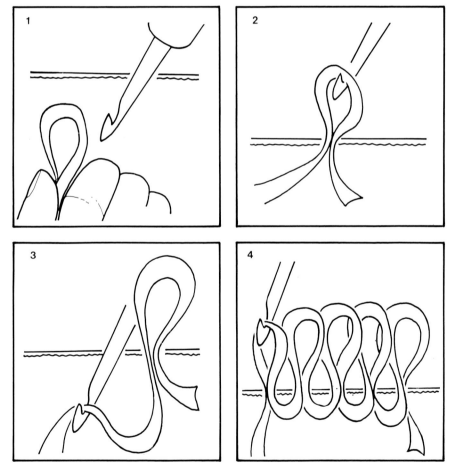

4
FELTING
TECHNIQUES

Although felt dates back to 6500BC, in modern times it has been greatly neglected, most of us today thinking of it as something we played with during our childhood. The process of felt making was first discovered in Asia, where Turkoman nomads produced the material for use in tent making. It is believed that it was brought to Britain by the Romans. Its versatile qualities have meant that it has survived as a useful textile right up to the present day.

Felt is produced by rubbing woollen fibres together; water is used as a lubricant, and this causes the wool to matt. Such a simple process can be easily performed by hand, and there is little difficulty in adapting it for machine production. Aesthetically, felt provides the perfect base for experimentation with mark making, pattern and colour. Its densely matted structure gives it insulating properties, so that it is a cosy, warm and sound-absorbing material which has the additional advantage of being very hard-wearing.

During the 1970s a travelling exhibition, "The Art of the Feltmaker", acted as a trigger for the contemporary appreciation of felt as a material and the revived interest in its design possibilities. Today's felt makers in India and the Middle East still follow the ancient methods, but it was their exotic use of Oriental dyes which attracted most attention in their section of the exhibition. They showed that the door was open to almost infinite experimentation in the realm of colours for those who were willing and inspired to take up the challenge. Among the modern British designers who have indeed been willing and inspired are Annie Sherburne and Janice Salmon, whose work is illustrated in this chapter.

While felt rugs should not be placed where excessive wear is likely, a reasonable amount of walking on them just continues the mechanical process of bonding the fibres. Balls of fluff that accumulate can easily be removed. They can be cleaned quite simply using light applications of carpet cleaner, and the colours are fast.

BASIC TECHNIQUES

The end product of felting is as various as the colours of wool used by the designer to make it. Because the process of felting does not mute or lessen the colour, quite striking bold and simple designs can be successfully created.

The textural possibilities of felt depend on the degree of mechanical agitation to which the fibres are subjected. It can have a loosely "woven" texture, in which the strands are individually visible, or it can have a much heavier, denser mass. The ability to mould and shape the material means that felt is successfully used in other fields, such as millinery.

Contemporary British rug makers use variations on two basic techniques. One process involves building up the matted structure without the aid of a neutral base. The coloured woollen fibres constitute the whole of the fabric, resulting in a greater depth of colour. The pattern is inlaid within each layer of matted fibres. If more pattern is to be built in, layers of varying colour can then be applied.

The alternative method, as used by both Annie Sherburne and Janice Salmon (see below), is to work on a neutral base of felt. On this surface of white wool, marks can be made using woollen fibres of different colours. When the whole is felted the result is a dense, strong surface, with the pattern and the base bonded together to form what has now become essentially a single piece of fabric.

GALLERY OF DESIGNERS

Annie Sherburne

Much of Annie Sherburne's work has been in the field of hats and accessories. On a larger scale, however, she has been expressing her gestural style in a range of colourful, decorative and contemporary rugs. Her themes and inspiration have their roots in many different cultures and periods. Her decorative ideas owe much to the Arts and Crafts movement as well as to the more recent explosive-colour ideas of 20th-century painting.

This felt rug, which can be used on the floor or as a wall-hanging, is "Soho Stroll" by Annie Sherburne.

Strong shapes and colours are used in another felt rug by Annie Sherburne, ''Mermaid''

Annie considers her approach to felted rugs to be like ''painting with wool''. To achieve her effect she works with marks made using coloured woollen fibres laid down on a white woollen base. During the machine process which follows, the fibres are agitated and start moving independently, effecting tiny ''tacking stitches''. The fabric becomes denser and stronger as the mechanical agitation intensifies, and the surface colours bond with the base to become part of it.

Sensual, colourful and decorative, Annie Sherburne's rugs look lovely on the wall, although the pieces have been milled to a density that makes it just as practical to use the rugs for the floor. They look at their best when they are used in ''special'' places, perhaps to enhance a seating area beneath a beautiful glass-topped coffee table, or by the hearth or in the bedroom.

Although she intends to continue making one-off pieces and to fulfil specific projects and commissions, Annie has been trying to make her work available to a wider public through increasing the quantities produced of each design and (partly as a consequence) decreasing the price to the individual purchaser. She has designed a system of production which will, she hopes, broaden the market for

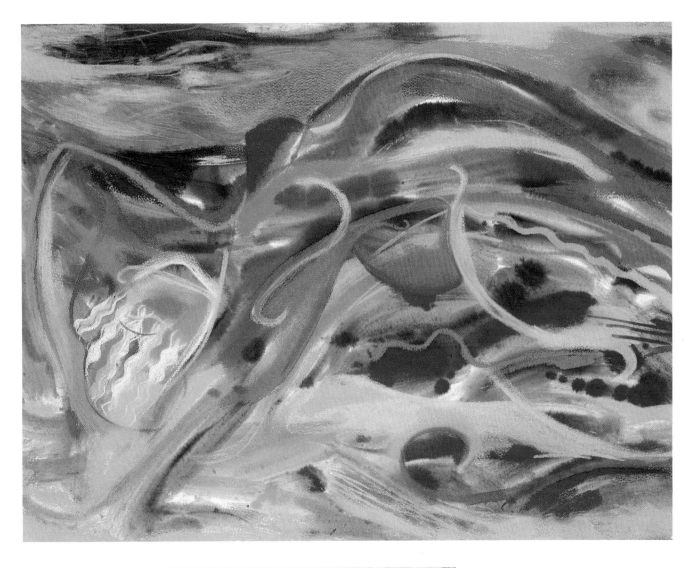

Above: Annie Sherburne uses her own pastel drawings as inspiration for many of her remarkable pieces in felt. *Left*: An explosion of shape and colour. Annie's felt works are never afraid to make a visual impact.

One of the colourful pastel drawings on which Annie Sherburne bases so many of her rug designs. Like many rug designers, Annie draws inspiration from her own work in the fine arts.

her works. A single design is reproduced several times over but, as the reproduction of the design is done by hand, each piece is part of a special edition and is in itself unique. After the design has been completed, the pieces are processed industrially. As each edition sells out, new work is added to what has become a continuously evolving range.

Janice Salmon

Janice Salmon uses industrial machinery to make her rugs. Her work is largely monotone and has a striking simplicity, making the maximum use of a fleecy white background onto which she ''draws'' her patterns and images using coloured wools. She patterns her rugs with recurring themes such as diagonal lines, diamond motifs and the

A felt rug by Janice Salmon, using black coils on a white background.

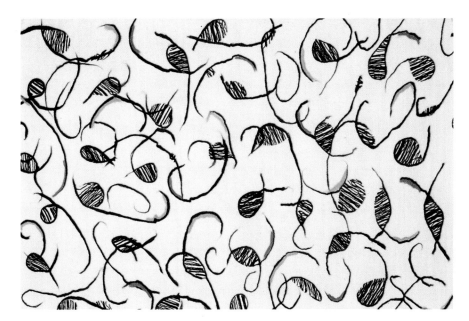

Left: This felt rug by Janice Salmon is in black and white and has an abstract ''leaf'' design repeated all over. *Below*: A detail of another black-and-white rug designed by Janice.

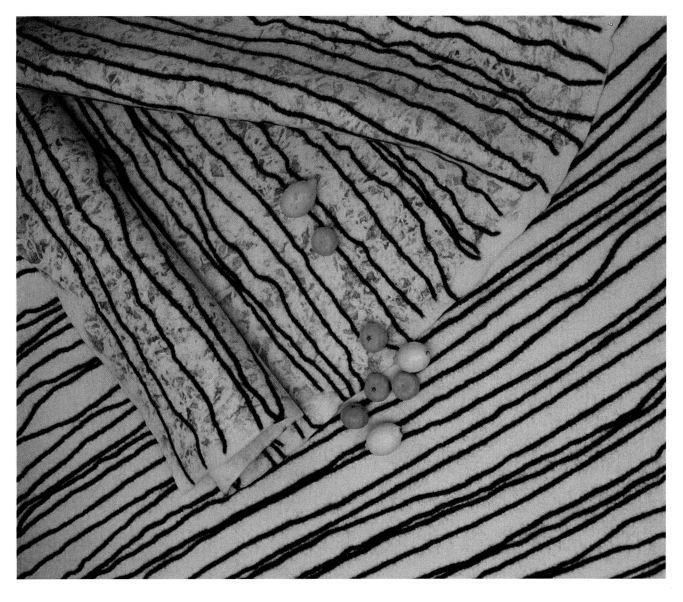

swirling shapes that make the designs easily recognizable as hers. Her work has always been built up with a high regard for the mechanical process, relying on the movement of the fibres to create her effects.

As an extension of her work with felt, she also makes fine papers, again using the malleable characteristics of the fibrous medium; she moulds the resulting material into bold shapes.

PROJECT

MAKING YOUR OWN FELT

Making felt is easy, and so you shouldn't allow the opportunity to maintain complete control over your rug design to be passed by. It is obviously a good idea to experiment with smaller tasks to find out what effects can be achieved before you move on to grander things.

You will need
- undyed fleece
- a pillow-case
- carders
- calico (muslin), canvas or cotton
- scissors
- needle and thread
- kettle
- liquid soap or acetic acid (white vinegar)
- rolling pin
- apron
- rubber gloves
- wooden board

Method

Washing
Untreated fleeces contain dirt and (possibly live) debris, and so they have to be washed. If the fleece you have bought has already been carded it will look more like lengths of hair (slivers) or cotton wool. Washing fleece should be done gently, as at this stage you want to avoid matting. Soak the fleece in warm water, squeeze it, and then place it in hot (not boiling) soapy water for one hour. Rinse the fleece in several batches of clean water, each a little cooler than the one before; keep on going until the fleece is clean and soap-free. Do not dry the fleece using direct heat. A successful way of drying it is to put it in a large pillow-case and then into the spin dryer.

Untangling the Fleece
Unscoured fleece has matted fibres, debris and knots that you will have to remove by pulling the fibres apart. Ideally the fleece will then be more voluminous, light and fluffy.

''Horse'', a handmade felt rug by Karen McCormac which uses embroidery to emphasize some of the motifs.

Carding

Mark your pair of carders ''left'' and ''right'', and use them in those hands in order to avoid any matting that might arise from mixing the mechanical processes each of them is used to perform. Place a handful of fibres across the left-hand carder (assuming you are right-handed) and then place the right-hand carder squarely on top. Keep your left hand still and pull the right-hand carder evenly across the lower one. Repeat the process until the fleece looks flat. Remove the fibres by placing the handle edge of the right-hand carder on the outside edge of the left-hand carder.

Layering the Fleece

Decide on the size of the piece of felt you want to make. One piece of hand-carded fleece measures about 7.5cm/3in square. Take a piece of calico (muslin), canvas or cotton the same width as the size of felt you require and twice the length, plus an allowance all round – about 7.5cm/3in for a piece of felt about 30cm/1ft square. Put the cloth on a flat surface, ideally a board, and place carded pieces side by side, all lying in the same direction, across half the length of the cloth. Once you have finished this first layer, put down another one on top of it but with the fibres at an angle of 90° to those of the first. Slight over-lapping will prevent gaps. Build up as many layers in this way as you need to make the thickness of felt you require; test this by compress-ing the layers with your fingers. Making the layers using slithers is done in the same way, not forgetting that the line of each layer should be at 90° to that of the layer preceding it.

Once you have built up as many layers as you need, fold the excess material over them and tack the package together close to the fleece. For larger pieces of work it is a good idea to tack diagonal rows across the work to keep the fibres from moving unevenly.

The Hardening Stage

The hardening process turns the fibres into a fused material. The less the fibres are disturbed at this stage the better. Place the package, preferably on a board, in the sink or other vessel that you plan to use for the immersion. Gradually spread hot or boiling water over the package. Wearing rubber gloves to protect your hands from the hot water, press the fibres lightly so that the water is allowed to soak through them thoroughly. At this stage you can spread the liquid soap or acetic acid over the fibrous parcel, after which you should add a little more water. Continue to compress the fibres by pressing them evenly. As the water cools, drain it off. Roll out the excess water with a rolling pin. Gently pour on some more hot water and repeat the process for about 15–20 minutes.

To check that the hardening process is complete, undo a corner of the calico (muslin) parcel and look at the fibres to see if they are starting to combine. If you have coarse fleece, this process may take as long as an hour. Remove the calico (muslin) covering as soon as the fibres start to enmesh themselves with it. If further binding is still necessary, the fibres can be loosely wrapped in the material as you continue the fusing process.

When making a large expanse of felt it may be a good idea to walk on the felting package. Don't start doing this until after the fibres have become reasonably compressed. Use one foot at a time to continue a smooth pressing motion.

Milling

The milling process begins once you have removed the covering and the fibres are fairly matted; the aim of the process is to make the fibres start to shrink so that they form your piece of felt. The process can take anywhere from 15 minutes to an hour, but there is no reason why you shouldn't take rest-breaks during it.

Continue draining away cold water and sprinkling with hot. Roll the felt, loosely wrapped in the cotton (muslin), backwards and forwards, periodically rotating the piece through 90°, aiming for an even texture – rather as if you were working with pastry. Rubbing the material between your thumb and forefinger will tell you when the felt is finished. When the fibres no longer slip you can move on to the drying stage.

Drying
Once the fibres are perfectly bonded together, place the piece in a pillow-case in the spin dryer or just roll it until no more water comes out. Dry it finally by leaving it flat, perhaps pinned to a board, in a warm place. For a smooth appearance you can steam-iron the felt.

Dyeing Your Own Fleece
Further to imprint your own hallmark on your felt, you can take on the messy art of dyeing. You will probably find that chemical dyes are more appropriate for your needs than natural ones, for a number of reasons. First, suitable natural dyes are often available only in large quantities for commercial use, whereas chemical dyes are easy to come by. A second problem with natural dyes concerns colour- and light-fastness; moreover, you must avoid dyes that would require you to soak the fleece in hot water for a long period.

Test the dyeing process beforehand on a small piece of fleece. Remember that, if there is any uncertainty about the desired result, you should start with light colours.

Making Felt with Dyed Fleece
A simple way of making good use of dyed fleece is to build up the layers of felt using different colours of fleece. If you carefully think out the colours to build up on top of each other you can achieve some very subtle colouring effects. By way of contrast, precisely arranged juxtapositioning of pieces of fleece can produce some stunningly vivid arrangements. Clearly it is simple to produce felt which is of a different colour on each side.

Combining colours can be done in the same way as mixing paints on a palette; for example, alternating layers of blue and yellow can produce an even green, while carding blue and yellow together can be used to create more varied or mottled effects. The range of colouring effects you can create is almost limitless. The best way to find out what you can do is to experiment using small quantities.

Other Effects
You can use different kinds of fleece to produce a type of variegated effect. Mixing long-staple fleece, short-staple fleece and curly fleece

can be done in various different ways to produce contrasting effects. For example, you can produce an intriguing texture by using a coarse short-staple fleece on what might be the base of a piece and a layer of long, curly fleece on the top.

The felt-making process has almost infinite versatility. Why not try using threads, yarns, feathers, pieces of raffia, inks and so on? You can introduce these at any stage of the process to create different effects. Some of your experiments will, obviously, be disastrous, but others will allow your imagination and creativity full rein.

Fleeces

The most obvious place to buy a fleece is at a sheep farm, but of course you may not be lucky enough to live near one. Alternatively, a good crafts shop should be able to supply you with a fleece, but once again you may have no such shop in your area. If need be, resort to the telephone. Crafts shops picked out of the Yellow Pages or from the list at the back of this book will tell you if they can help or possibly put you on to someone who can. Guilds of craftsmen and spinners will likewise be able to help with information. Although it may be a time-consuming process tracking down a supplier, remember that you will have to do it only once!

When you are learning, all you need is a small quantity of fleece to play with. If you plan to embark on a rug, though, you will need a whole fleece. Scoured or carbonized fleece is easier to deal with because it has already been washed, treated and sorted into a uniform quality. If, however, you are using an untreated fleece direct from a farm you have to sort out the different qualities of fibres into piles; for felt-making you should ideally use the least matted, softest areas.

The appearance of sorted fleeces varies depending on how they have been carded. For felt-making the ideal is a short staple (fibre-length), of about 2.5cm/1in, and a high count (fineness of fibre), of about 60. However, you may alter your preference in these respects as a result of experience.

Carders

Carders are used to remove tangles and debris so that your fleece can be combed into parallel strands. Carders are essential when working with untreated fleeces. For the beginner, hand carders, as used by spinners, are perfectly adequate; you should be able to buy them from the good crafts shop you located when buying your fleece.

Carders are available both flat and rounded – choose whichever type you prefer. A drum carder is rather different, and is used for working on a large scale. If necessary, seek the advice of your crafts shop.

5

WOVEN AND
TAPESTRY RUGS

The process of weaving is far older than history, and is found in every culture in the world, from the most traditional to the most sophisticated. The oldest hand looms of which we know were already quite advanced devices, using systems of cords and rods to enable the weaver to pass the weft threads through the warp threads in groups rather than singly. By the Middle Ages people were using treadle-operated looms which could be "programmed" to weave repeated patterns in the cloth – indeed, these were probably the most complicated of any type of machine used during the Middle Ages and the Renaissance. Power looms began to appear at the end of the 18th century, and not long afterwards J.-M. Jacquard developed a punched-card system which allowed patterns to be woven automatically. Since then all commercial weaving in the developed societies has been done automatically.

However, machine-produced cloth lacks much of the charm, texture and one-off brilliance that can be achieved using the hand loom. Nowhere is this more true than in the field of rug making.

WOVEN RUGS

The first point to remember about woven rugs is that the finished product is as much concerned with the process of weaving as with the design. This can be seen as a limitation, in that the rug maker's designs are restricted by the equipment and materials used. Conversely, though, there is a quality about a woven rug which cannot be achieved by any other means. In this woven rugs differ from those made using tapestry weaving (see page 74), where the techniques used are governed by the desired image.

BASIC TECHNIQUES

When we look closely at any woven material we find that it is made up of two sets of interlaced threads. These are known as the warp and the weft. The warp is the set of threads running vertically through the weaving; the fabric is, essentially, constructed on the warp. The word "warp" comes from the fact that, during the weaving process, these threads are warped or stretched. The weft threads lie at right angles to those of the warp. They are carried by the shuttle and interlace with the warp threads to form the width of the cloth. Because of the tension placed on them the warp yarns need to be generally harder, finer and more tightly spun than those of the weft. Cotton and linen are the two most popular fibres used for warp threads. Weft yarns, by contrast, can be made of practically any material, from the wholly natural through to the purely synthetic – although mixtures of the two do not usually sit well together.

The simplest way to weave a rug or tapestry is by using a weaving frame. These can be bought or made quite cheaply (see pages 41–2). There are two types of frame relevant in our current context, the two being distinguished by the different ways in which the warp can be attached to the frame.

A fixed-warp frame is one to which the warp is fastened directly, providing a fixed area, about two-thirds the length of the frame, in which the piece can be worked. In the tensioned-warp frame, by contrast, the warp is attached to two rods and then wrapped around the frame, the tension being achieved by drawing the two rods together behind the frame by means of a strong cord or – in the case of larger frames which are themselves fixed firmly to a wall or other rigid structure – through the use of a screw or tourniquet mechanism. The advantage of this latter method is that you can draw the warp over the frame and so be able to weave a piece that is longer than the frame itself.

Whatever type of frame you use, make sure that it is at least 15cm/6in longer and 5cm/2in wider than the final dimensions of the rug you wish to weave.

There are two other items of equipment you need aside from your frame: the shed stick and the shuttle stick. The shed is the space between the alternating warp threads through which the weft yarn is passed. The shed stick is used to separate the alternate warps, so as to create that space. The shuttle stick is flat and is the same length and width as the warp; it has a notch cut at each end. You use the shuttle stick to bring the weft yarn through the shed.

The yarns you use for the warp must be strong, since they will be held permanently under tension. They need also to be smooth: hairy warp yarns tend to stick together and thus are difficult to separate.

The weft threads are woven in from both right and left. You can weave different textures of fabric by using different thicknesses of

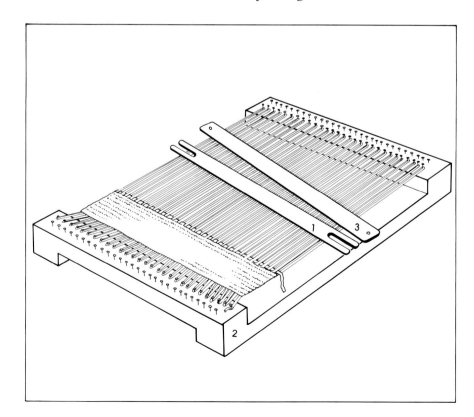

A simple fixed-warp weaving frame. 1 The shuttle stick. 2 The frame. 3 The shed stick. See text for further explanation.

warp and weft threads and by changing the positioning of the shed stick. To finish off you remove the work from the frame either by simply unhooking it or by cutting the warp yarn at both ends.

GALLERY OF DESIGNERS

Alice Clark

Alice Clark weaves colourful rugs for contemporary interiors. She has developed her warp-faced rugs in a highly original way. Her rugs, whose designs range from the strongly geometric to the somewhat asymmetric, are both functional and innovative. Her craft-oriented techniques allow her exciting variations on strongly linear patterns.

Her work differs from that of many other rug weavers in that she uses warp-faced, rather than the more customary weft-faced, weaves. In most woven rugs the visible surface is composed of the weft threads, but in a warp-faced rug the warp threads completely hide the weft threads and thereby comprise the surface of the piece. This variation completely changes the structural appearance of the rug. The warp yarns used are thicker and more closely set than those used in weft-faced designs. Warp-faced weaves are normally arrangements of stripes in various colours of yarn, although multicoloured yarns can be used.

Susan Foster

Susan Foster is a largely self-taught rug weaver. Energy and determination, coupled with endless enthusiasm – these are the ingredients which have enabled Susan successfully to produce her stunningly bold creations. Although she taught herself to weave by attending courses with master craftsmen, she has since been able to pass on the fruits of her growing knowledge and experience to others – as well

Opposite above: Alice Clark's warp-faced woven rugs are in vivid and subtle colourings.

Opposite below: Brilliant tones of blue predominate in this woven rug with tassels, designed by Alice Clark.

Below left: In her woven rugs Susan Foster subtly combines pattern and colour, as we can see in this example. *Below right*: Shades of blue and violet are woven onto a white background in this rug designed by Susan Foster. Like Sara Parnell (see pages 45–6) and many other designers, Susan often draws inspiration from Navajo rugs.

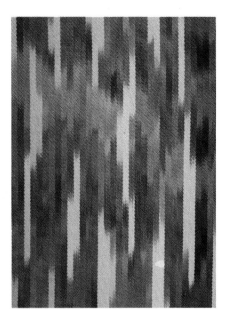

Opposite above: This flat-weave tapestry rug by Lesley Millar has a small repeating background design with a strong central geometric motif in bright primary colours.
Opposite below: Another flat-weave tapestry rug by Lesley Millar. Woven in bright pastels, this rug has a small repeating geometric border and large flat shapes in the central area.

Here Lesley Millar has used the colours of the interior as a starting point when creating her geometrically designed woven rug.

as, of course, applying them to her own designs. She has gone from running a very individual shop in the dining room of her home in Kendal to marketing her inspirational creations internationally.

She is keen on both technical perfection and experimentation. She has tried Navajo-type twill rugs, "pick and pick" rag and wool rugs, and *krokgrag* designs which explore the possibilities of rich Persian-like themes. Inspired by stained-glass windows, she combines making rag rugs with weaving in wool, sometimes framing areas of one technique inside the other. Her priority is to develop colour and texture together in harmony. She draws her inspiration from whatever she sees around her, from the Midnight Sun depicted in old Finnish rugs to the visual decorations of Hindu temples.

Lesley Millar

Leslie Millar's rugs have added exciting stretches of colourful geometry to private collections in the United Kingdom, Germany and

the United States. She makes exciting flat-weave tapestry rugs from 100 per cent wool, using linen or cotton warps. Working mainly to commission, she enjoys the challenge of meeting the often exacting requirements of customers while yet remaining true to her own design preoccupations. The greatest reward, she finds, is seeing the way in which her very individual productions stand out against the backdrop of mass-produced textiles that have little to offer in the way of self-expression. Also she enjoys having such a personal involvement with her clients and the exercise of designing and making something directly tailored to specific briefs and room settings. She dyes all her wools herself, so that she can make extremely versatile use of colours. She can thus design rugs to accord with particular colour schemes secure in the knowledge that she will be able to reproduce precisely the colours she has envisaged.

Anne Mulcahy

Anne Mulcahy's work is halfway between weaving and tapestry: it is not so repetitious as pure weaving but it is less discontinuous than pure tapestry.

Some of her rugs are precisely designed before the weaving begins. These designs are weft-faced pieces, and the end product is a flat, even surface based strongly on colour, uniformity of weave and clarity of outline.

Designs that are not so strictly planned in advance are, in the case of rugs, produced from weft-faced weaves, but in the case of wall hangings they may also be even-weaves. These more spontaneous designs have a strong sense of shape and individual character. Decisions about changes in colour, and in combinations of colours, are taken as the work progresses; such decisions may affect either the

A striped, weft-faced woven rug by Anne Mulcahy. Anne has taken great advantage of the use of deliberately positioned, colourful geometric shapes.

wool being wound onto the shuttles or the number of shuttles being manipulated across the line of weave.

Anne enjoys the freedom of switching from one weaving approach to another in order to keep her inspiration shining through introducing variety to her work. She likes every piece to encapsulate a new idea, and so no two items of her work are ever identical. Her enthusiasm is fuelled by the mental stimulation of designing and the physical enjoyability of making her rugs and wall hangings.

A black, grey and white weft-faced woven rug with a white "swirl" motif. This example again shows off the verve of Anne Mulcahy's design work.

Sophie Pattinson

Sophie Pattinson designs and makes woven rugs and wall coverings using a variety of materials including wool, linen and cotton – as well as, frequently, incorporating painted strips of wood in her work. Her designs are brightly coloured linear patterns with occasional coloured swirls. Many of her designs are highly symmetrical, but others contain abstract features of line and shape.

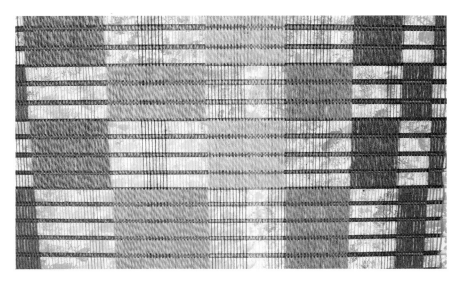

Another rug woven by Sophie Pattinson. Here she has used a repeating geometric motif with gradations of colour.

A woven rug by Sophie Pattinson, made in a mixture of wool, linen and cotton.

TAPESTRY WEAVING

Tapestry weaving can be regarded as a halfway stage between pure tapestry and pure weaving: it is neither, but shares many similarities with each of them. The process is frequently used by designers who are concerned more with the quality of the finished image than with the niceties of the techniques used to produce it.

Tapestry weave is worked in small areas at a time on a frame or a loom; this allows greater freedom to build up a design horizontally. The technique is ideal for intricate designs in which you want to show fine detail. It is often used as a way of translating paintings into tapestry, as epitomized by the work of Dilys Stinson (see pages 82–4). Tapestry weave uses basic equipment and simplified weaving techniques to achieve strong images.

TAPESTRY RUGS

Tapestry is often confused with needlepoint. Rugs which use a canvas backing – such as the rug by Julia Milne which we set out at the end of this chapter – are technically needlepoint but are generally described as tapestries. The confusion extends far further than this; for example, the Bayeux Tapestry is in fact, because it is worked on canvas, in actuality a needlepoint. Clearly the definitions are very confused, and so in this chapter we consider the two techniques as if they were one.

BASIC TECHNIQUES

Tapestry or needlepoint rugs are worked on a canvas backing, with either rug wool or tapestry wool being used double. You can buy canvas in various densities from 1.5–2 meshes per centimetre/$3\frac{1}{3}$–5 meshes per inch. When you buy canvas be sure to check out certain details – for example, make sure that the mesh is regular and that it contains no joined or weakened threads. If possible choose a canvas with a shiny or waxy surface, as this finish will provide additional strength and protection against wear and tear.

The stitches are worked using an ordinary tapestry needle, but make sure that the eye is large enough for the wool to pass through it with ease. You can if you want work the rug in a frame, but this is not absolutely necessary.

When you prepare to work the rug, and before you cut the canvas, plan the shape and size that you require and then allow a 5cm/2in margin all round. The selvedges are usually at the sides of the rug. Before you start to work the design, bind the raw edges to prevent fraying; to do this you can use masking tape, sticky tape or bias binding, or alternatively you can turn back the raw edges and slip-stitch them down. As with the planning, you should decide upon and carry out the edge finish before you begin to work on the rug.

The most commonly used stitch is the tent stitch, and there are two methods of executing it. The first and more straightforward method is worked in rows from right to left. The second – the diagonal method – produces a heavier and more hard-wearing backing.

Most patterns for tapestry rugs are worked from charts drawn on squared paper. Each square represents one mesh on the canvas, and each symbol represents a different colour. Work should start in the top right-hand corner. The wool should be cut into lengths, about 45cm/18in long; don't break the wool, as this will cause it to stretch.

To start off, leave a 2.5cm/1in length of wool at the back of the canvas, and work it over as you go along. As you stitch, be careful not to pull the wool too tightly, and try to maintain an even tension. Don't allow the wool to become twisted, as this will result in thin patches; if the wool does begin to twist, drop the threaded needle and allow the wool to untwist naturally.

On finishing a thread or section of colour, weave the wool through a few stitches on the underside of the work and cut it close to where it emerges, so that you keep the wrong side of the work neat. If you make a mistake, carefully unpick or cut the stitches, making sure that as you do so you don't damage or distort the canvas. Use a fresh strand of wool to restart the work – don't be tempted to reuse unpicked yarn, as it will not produce even stitches.

Unless you are using a frame, roll the canvas out of the way as the work progresses, so that it is easier to handle. If you're making a large rug you can do it in sections which you can join up afterwards.

Once you have completed the work you may well find that it has been distorted away from the correct shape. If so, you must block it: be reassured that, no matter how badly the rug has been distorted, it can be successfully blocked back into shape. Before you start blocking, use carbon tetrachloride or water to treat any soiled areas, working with a clean cloth.

For the process of blocking, first cover a flat wooden surface (such as a board) with a large sheet of clean paper. Onto this, mark the precise size and shape of the rug, using a setsquare to ensure right angles at the corners. Unless you have incorporated a pile stitch into the design, place the tapestry right-side-down (or right-side-up if you have incorporated a pile stitch) on the marked paper, securing it in place with drawing pins spaced 1–2cm/$\frac{1}{2}$–$\frac{3}{4}$in apart. If the wool is not colour-fast, apply a solution of salt and water and leave it to dry; if, on the other hand, it is colour-fast, thoroughly wet the rug with cold water and, once again, leave it to dry. If the work is badly distorted, repeat this procedure as often as need be.

Once you have finished blocking, finish the edges by trimming the margins of the canvas to 2.5cm/1in; turn this under and tack in place.

There are two ways of finishing the rug. The first uses rug binding. With the wrong edge of the rug uppermost, sew one edge of the binding to the folded edge of the canvas and the other to the back of the rug, encasing the raw edges and mitring the corners. The other technique is to back the rug with a lining. Cut the lining to the size of the rug plus a 2.5cm/1in hem allowance all round. Turn the hem allowance to the wrong side and mitre the corners; use carpet thread to slip-stitch the lining to the rug.

Alternatives to the tent stitch. *Above*: The cross stitch. **1** Work from right to left. Bring the needle out from the bottom line and form the stitch diagonally upwards towards the left. Bring the needle out once more directly beneath where the first stitch was pushed through. Continue in this way until you have a row of diagonal stitches. **2** Complete the crosses by working a row of diagonal stitches in the opposite direction. *Below*: The horizontal tent stitch. This is a very small stitch and, because it covers both sides of the work equally, gives a hardwearing result.
1 Work from right to left. Bring the needle up through the fabric and then push it back through the next intersection to the upper right. Bring the needle up through the next intersection to the left of the starting point. **2** At the end of the row, insert the needle as if to complete a further stitch. **3** Turn the work completely around and work the next row back from right to left (i.e., in the opposite direction to the original).

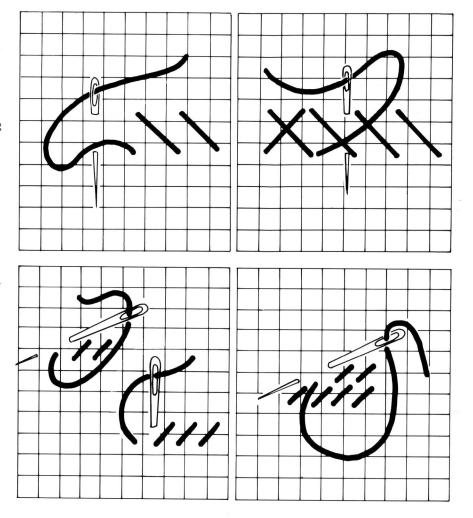

If you make a rug in sections which then have to be joined up, make sure that each piece of canvas is of the same weight and mesh-size. Leave 5cm/2in from the edges to be joined as you work each section. Block each piece individually before you join them all together. As you work the individual sections, allow for the fact that you will need to work five pattern rows over the joined edges. Once you start to join two of the edges, trim away all but four rows of unworked mesh on one of them. Place the cut edge of the mesh over the remaining section of the work, matching the pattern and the unworked meshes of the two sections. Using large pins, pin the two pieces together through the centres of the lapped edges. Work five rows of pattern through both layers of the canvas. Trim away any threads of canvas that are still exposed.

If you want you can incorporate needlepoint stitches other than the tent stitch. However, before you work them into the rug, test them on a scrap of canvas to make sure that they are suitable and that they cover the canvas adequately. A couple of alternative stitches are shown in the diagrams on page 76.

Rya and Flossa Rugs

Rya rugs have become incredibly popular today. There are two main techniques of making rya rugs, one of which is really a variant of hand tufting and so is discussed on page 95. Both techniques use the same principle: that one is working with a bundle of yarns of different, although possibly related, colours. The knotting method is essentially the same as for the hand-tufted rug detailed on pages 94–5, but there are two distinct differences: first, the rows on the canvas are further apart; second, the strands of yarn are much longer (the longer pile gives the shaggy appearance, as opposed to the short flat tufts of the hand-tufted rug). Rya hand-hooking is a much quicker method, both because three or more strands are hooked at the same time and because the longer strands of yarn cover up the canvas more swiftly.

The technique of rya knotting is often thought of as being a modern discovery because of the recent upsurge of interest in it. But it is far from new – indeed, it is millennia old, the oldest surviving example of the technique dating back to 500BC. Rya knotting almost certainly originated many centuries before even this date, and probably first emerged in Central Asia. From here it spread westwards to Scandinavia thanks to the explorations of the Vikings.

The rugs are characteristically brightly coloured and have an immediate visual impact, an effect created by the careful selection and positioning of similarly toned shades, very often using simple abstract designs. A variation is the flossa rug. Although, the two terms are sometimes used to mean the same thing, and although the same knot – the Ghiordes knot (see page 78) – is in both cases used to produce the loops, there is in fact a subtle difference. The rows of knots in a flossa rug are placed close together to produce a firm

Making the Ghiordes knot. 1 Working from the right side, pass the threaded needle down through the backing canvas and back up through the adjacent shed. 2 Pass the needle down past the other adjacent warp thread and then back up to the right side. Hold the loop to the desired length with your thumb and pull the knot tight. 3 and 4 Repeat the knot, working across the row. Once the row has been completed, work along the one above it, and so on. When you've finished the knotting, cut away the tops of the loops to create the final pile.

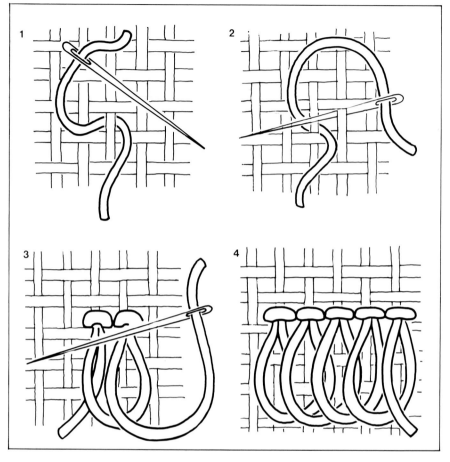

vertical pile which has a soft luxuriant surface. In a rya rug, by contrast, the knots are spaced more widely apart so that the tufts lie flatter, giving a rougher, shaggier finish.

Traditionally both types of rugs were woven on a loom. However, a special foundation fabric has now become available. It has a sort of latticework construction (see diagram on page 79) which makes working the rug easier.

Ghiordes knots are made using a large-eyed needle which has been threaded with up to six strands of either tapestry wool or lightweight rug wool, usually in several closely related shades. The number of needles used depends upon the number of different colour combinations within the rug.

The technique is reasonably simple (see diagrams on page 78). The work begins at the bottom left-hand selvedge. The first space in the backing canvas is skipped and the needle is passed through the second space and then, from left to right, back up through the first until a loose end of yarn is left poking out from the second space; this loose end should be the same length as the desired pile – or longer, as it can be trimmed later. This loose end is held firmly in place below the row using the fingers and thumb. The needle is then passed through the third space and back up through the second; the yarns are pulled tight to form the knot. The needle is next passed through the fourth space and back up through the third, until there is a loop

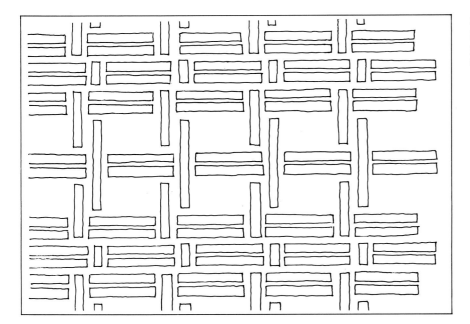

Rya canvas. Unlike latch-hook canvas, this has open mesh only on alternate rows. The pile is so long that in the finished work the canvas is completely covered.

the required depth of the final pile left on the right side. This loop is held, as before, below the row by the fingers and thumb while the needle is taken down through the fifth space and back up through the fourth, the yarns are pulled tight, and the knot is formed. This process continues along the row, each loop being as near as possible the same size. (Some rug makers work the loops over a ruler in order to ensure that they are indeed all the same size, but many prefer to do without this guide, reckoning that minor variations in pile-depth are actually desirable because they disguise any ridges there might be in the finished article.) The final space in each row remains unworked. After each row has been completed, the rug maker cuts through the loops.

Should the rug maker wish to change colour in the middle of a row, he or she works as before up to the colour change. The remaining end of yarn is then cut to the desired length of pile. Work is started with the new colour in the same way as at the beginning of the rug making.

Once the work has been completed, there are various ways of finishing the two short edges of the rug.

One involves, first, unravelling the base fabric for about 7.5–10cm/ 3–4in, stopping at an openwork row. The weft threads are removed to leave a fringe of warp threads. With the wrong side uppermost, the fringed threads are knotted together in bunches of three, the knots being tightened close to the edge of the work. The third bunch of threads is brought under the second and then over, around and under the first, and finally over the second and under the fourth; the bunch is pinned to the base fabric. Now the first bunch is brought under the second, over the third and under the fourth to be pinned in place. This is continued until all the bundles of threads have been dealt with. Finally the rug maker uses a crochet hook to weave the threads in and out of the base fabric and trims the ends.

The other finishing technique produces a twisted fringe. After the main work has been completed, the weft threads up to the ninth row of the base fabric are cut and removed. The remaining warp threads are separated into groups of three. The first group of threads is knotted close to the edge of the work, as is the second. The two groups are twisted clockwise until they are tight, and then the second is placed over the first and the two groups are twisted anticlockwise until they are firmly twisted together. A knot is made at the outer end. This continues until all the threads have been twisted and knotted.

GALLERY OF DESIGNERS

Roger Oates and Fay Morgan

Of the two partners in Morgan & Oates, Fay uses hand weaving on a larger scale than does Roger; her technique is "more woven, less tapestry" when the intention is to produce a plurality of rugs with a

Below: Designed by Roger Oates and Fay Morgan, this flat-weave tartan rug is made from pure wool. *Opposite*: This gun-tufted rug, designed by Roger and Fay for the London headquarters of the Peat Marwick Group, reflects both the architecture and the interior.

A rag rug designed exclusively for the Designers Guild by Roger and Fay.

similar design. Roger's creations in tapestry weaving tend more to be one-offs; they are hand-woven in order to allow the precise detail of the designed image to have pride of place in the production process.

Together, Fay and Roger can produce woven textures combining dexterity in two areas so that the process of producing a finished design as close as possible to the original specifications in no way restricts the use of detail. Their joint experience with different raw materials – and the way that these work with different colours, shapes and pattern designs – means that they not only work with tapestry and pure new wool but also tuft and weave with cotton rags. In addition, they produce interior furnishings, from floor coverings to table linens.

Dilys Stinson

The modern intensity of Dilys Stinson's designs and the attention she gives to textural relief have attracted some of the many artists with whom she has worked – Henry Moore, Howard Hodgkin, Philip Sutton, Aileen Agar and Marta Rogoyska being among them.

Dilys Stinson specializes in flat-weave tapestry which, despite the fact that new weaving equipment is constantly being developed, is still best woven by hand. She works in the Gobelins tradition (see page 23), concerned with the particular qualities of the tapestry itself: intensity of colour and richness of texture. Her preoccupation with surface rather than line means that the personal hand-crafted approach is essential.

Planning the pattern in detail is extremely important when working in this medium. Dilys first works out her design on paper, paying careful attention to both colour and texture. Using handmade and commercially produced paper – some dyed, some painted, and

Opposite above: Another flat-weave rug by Dilys Stinson, "Caribbean Squares". Its technical excellence is matched only by the vivid colours that make up the five "paintings" which feature on the rug's textured background. *Opposite below*: "Elson's Rug", again by Dilys. The collage effect of this tapestry-weave rug gives us a glimpse of her technique of arranging torn coloured pieces of paper until she reaches a satisfactory design solution.

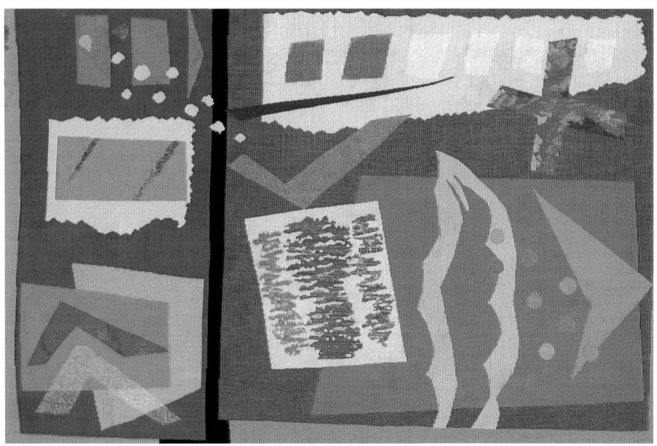

some cut and torn – she builds up a collage that she will be able to translate into the final woven image. To make the best use of texture, she uses different fibres to interpret the different surfaces of the paper – silk, cotton, linen and mohair, as well as the worsted more usually used for woven tapestry. The images vary between purely representative and totally abstract, allowing every viewer an independent interpretation. Her inspiration comes from many sources, but often the origin is a passing comment overheard in conversation.

Colour is the most important aspect of Dilys's work. She dyes 90 per cent of all the yarns she uses; by so doing she ensures not only perfect choice of colour but also certainty about light-fastness and a maximum choice in the quality of the yarns that she uses.

Dilys has been working on a series of designs based on calligraphic marks, cave paintings and hieroglyphics. As usual, her most recent works come in a variety of scales. She thinks of tapestry as a monumental art, believing that her designs are better on a larger scale; however, she makes smaller pieces as well, as she considers them to be more suitable for exhibition purposes.

Sue Beckett

Sue Beckett works with strong geometric designs. She makes her rugs from standard 80 per cent wool and 20 per cent nylon yarn on a cotton warp. She uses a simple upright frame rather than a loom, allowing herself the versatility required to produce her simplest bold

Reminiscent of skyscrapers, this woven rug by Sue Beckett has shades of blue and black as well as "windows" of colour.

designs in conjunction with her intricately detailed patterns of colour.

From her original wall-hanging tapestry designs she has worked downwards towards the floor. To complement the bold geometric shapes of her elevated wall-hangings she now makes rugs in standard carpet yarns. She works independently and to commission, always producing exclusive "one-off" designs. She sees an exciting future collaborating with interior designers and architects to create holistic interiors for private clients.

Kaffe Fassett

Kaffe Fassett's is now a household name among tapestry and knitting enthusiasts. He has achieved his current popularity through producing his designs in reproducible form, often as kits — these tend to be for his smaller designs, which are easier to produce commercially and hence more suitable for retailing. His talent for tapestry weaving is much more evident in his larger, individual pieces, in which he does not have to compromise his extensive use of colour and detail.

Kaffe's style is built upon his passion for colour and his love of paintings. He uses yarns as a painter would use threads of paint. His sources of inspiration for his floor coverings have included ancient mosaics and scenes far removed from his more commercially popular floral compositions.

It is not difficult to see how Kaffe's flair for painting combines with

This woven rug by Sue Beckett has large areas of flat colour interspersed with blocks of strong colours.

his talent for creating textiles to enhance his rug design. Size, texture and colour all work together to make the rug a perfect medium in which he can express images in textural form.

Opposite: Designed by Kaffe Fassett, this needlepoint rug – along with a matching cushion – can be bought in kit form.
Below: This canvaswork rug, designed by Julia Milne, uses tent stitch and is based on traditional floral motifs.

PROJECT

A NEEDLEPOINT RUG BY JULIA MILNE

This floral tapestry rug was designed by Julia Milne. Julia designs tapestry to order for private commissions or publication. She has

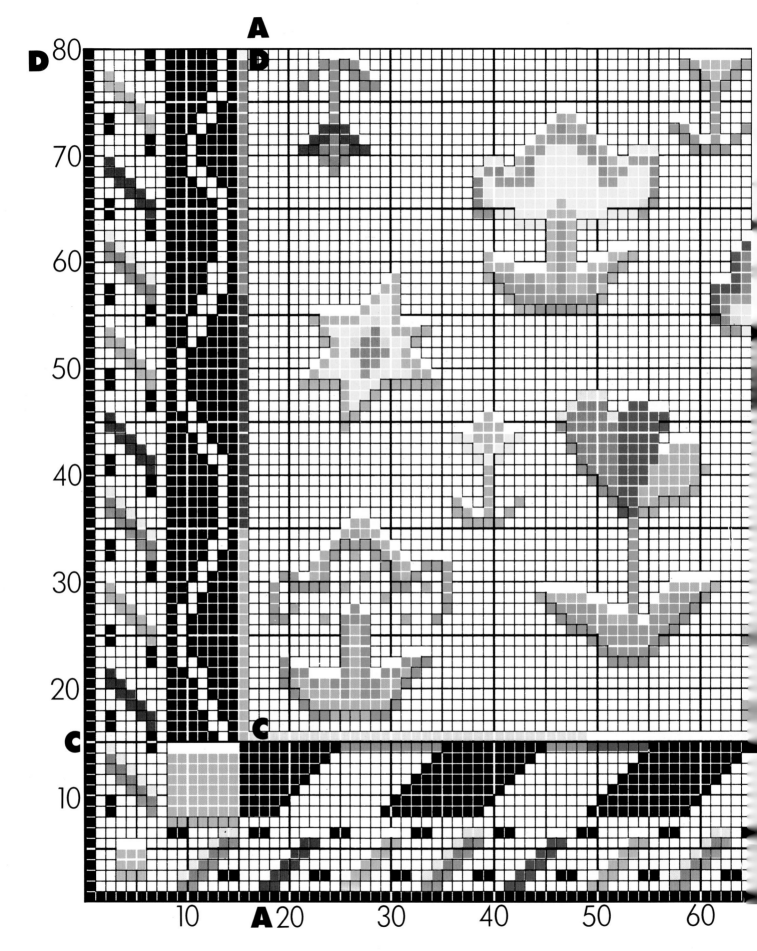

X **Work this motif on the left hand side only.** B

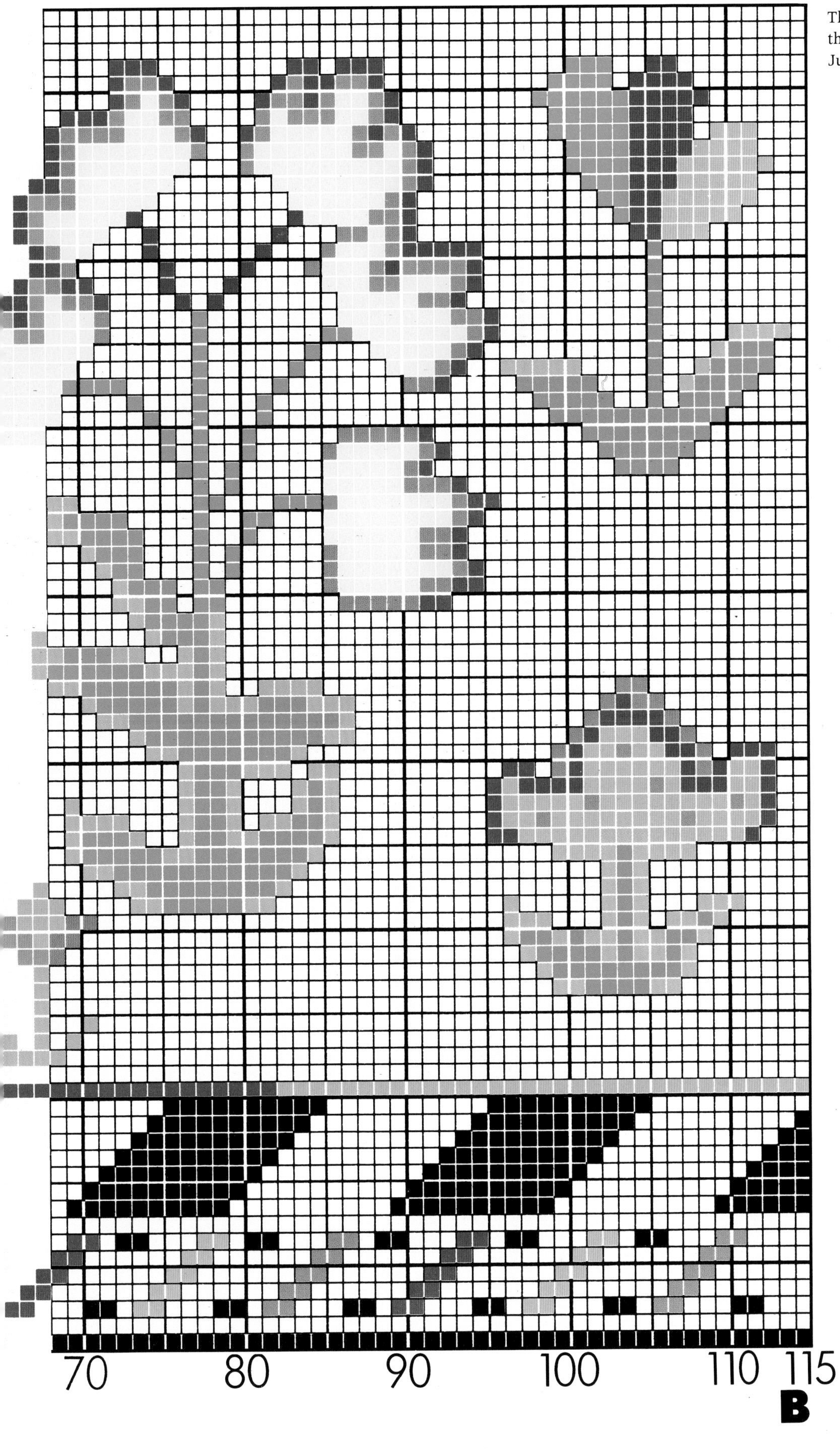

The chart to follow when making the needlepoint rug designed by Julia Milne.

70 80 90 100 110 115

B

A detail of the rug by Julia Milne, showing the canvas and the geometric border.

You Will Need
- 5-mesh plain rug canvas of dimensions 90 × 125cm/36 × 50in (finished size 80 × 120cm/32 × 46in)
- size 13 tapestry needle
- Readicut 6-ply rug wool (50g/2oz balls): 18 balls of lemon, 4 balls of black, 3 balls of white, 2 balls each of green, turquoise, dark pink, pink, yellow and gold, 1 ball of blue (the Readicut wool is available by mail order only from Readicut Wool Co. Ltd., Dept 1PN ED1, Terry Mills, Ossett, West Yorkshire WF5 9SA – when ordering quote no. 89995 "Julia"; if you can't get hold of the exact wool, improvise by comparison with the colours shown in the illustrations)

Method
If you have a large enough tapestry frame, then use it. If not, the rug can be worked successfully without a frame assuming that you take care and don't pull the wool too tight.

The rug is worked entirely in diagonal tent stitch. Start at the lower left-hand corner, using lengths of wool approximately 1m/40in long. Work the design as shown on the graph on pages 88–9, but do not fill in the background. When the first quarter is finished, work the diagonal border and flower motifs for the lower right-hand corner by repeating the section from line A/A to line B/B; then extend the vertical left-hand border by repeating the section from line C/C to line D/D. Finish the top left-hand corner and the turquoise square to correspond with the bottom left-hand corner.

Turn the canvas round and work the second half of the rug as described above. Work the motif marked "X" on the left-hand side of the rug only. When you have completed all the borders and motifs, work the background from the bottom left-hand corner, working in one direction diagonally across the rug.

The Tent Stitch

The tent stitch is one of the basic stitches used in canvas work. It can be worked in horizontal and vertical rows, but the diagonal tent stitch is preferable for this rug because it is less likely to distort the backing cloth. Tent stitch is known also as basketweave stitch because of the woven effect it produces on the wrong side.

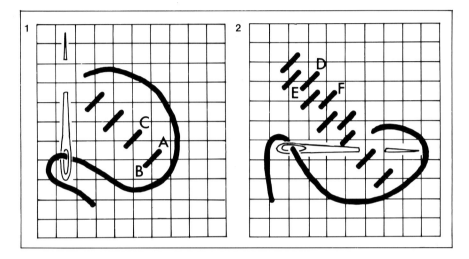

Working the tent stitch. **1** To begin, knot the wool and take the needle through to the wrong side of the work a short distance from the starting point. Bring the needle up through hole A. (The knot can be cut off when you have worked over the thread.) Re-insert the needle through B to form the first stitch. Counting two holes up from B bring the needle up through C ready to form the second stitch. Continue in this way until you come to the end of a diagonal row. **2** The second row is worked in the reverse direction. When you have completed the first row form the first stitch of the second by bringing the needle up through D and down through E. Then counting two holes along to the right (instead of vertically as for the first row) bring the needle up through F ready for the next stitch. Continue as shown, working in diagonal lines alternately up and down.

To begin you have to knot the wool and take the needle through to the wrong side of the work a short distance from the starting point. Bring the needle up through hole A. (Once you've worked over the thread you can cut off the knot.) Reinsert the needle through B to form the first stitch. Count two holes up from B to bring the needle up through C, ready to form the second stitch. Continue in this way until you come to the end of a diagonal row.

The second row is worked in the reverse direction. When you have completed the first row, form the first stitch of the second by bringing the needle up through D and down through E. Then, counting two holes along to the right (instead of vertically, as for the first row), bring the needle up through F, ready for the next row. Continue in this way, working in diagonal lines alternately up and down.

Finishing

Finish off all loose ends by darning them into the back of the work. Turn back the unworked canvas at the edges, catching it down to the back of the rug using a slip-stitch.

If the work has become distorted you will need to block it back into shape. Gently wet the back of the rug, using a sponge or a spray bottle, and pull it into the correct shape; then pin the edges down firmly onto a piece of plywood or hardboard, measuring from edge to edge to make sure that there is no distortion. By the time the rug has dried out naturally it should have become fixed into its proper shape.

If you wish, back the finished rug with a heavyweight cotton backing cloth.

Professional Tips
- If you don't have a frame on which to stretch the canvas, work the rug on a flat surface and secure it with weights to prevent distortion of the shape.
- The size of this rug may be a bit daunting for the beginner, but why not work a rug on this scale with a friend? The finished rug, done during the evenings alone, should take 2–4 weeks.
- It is easier to stitch one motif at a time and count the stitches for the next section of the pattern.
- Use the chart shown here to create your own designs. The motifs used in this rug can be utilized in a different pattern formation. Transfer them onto graph paper and then use your own design ideas!

6

TUFTED RUGS

Tufted rugs, made by looping yarn through a canvas backing and knotting it, have always been popular with designers. The technique allows very detailed work, gives you close control over production, and permits a vast and versatile range of patterns and designs to be executed.

BASIC TECHNIQUES

Hand-tufted Rugs

Hand tufting – and, for that matter, gun tufting (see below) – shares with tapestry weaving the advantage that the desired image can be carefully planned and drawn out on graph paper and then reproduced very accurately in the form of the finished rug. However, hand tufting allows you greater flexibility: you are not restricted by tapestry's need to use continuous threads, and so can indulge more in the impulsive building up of colour and style that is the hallmark of an evolving piece of work. Because tufted-rug designs can rely on the use of very fine detail, they are a popular choice among makers who have a specific or precisely detailed image in mind.

Hand-tufted rugs, often known as latch-hooked rugs, are worked using a canvas foundation and short lengths of rug yarn which are knotted into the canvas using a tool called a latch hook. Latch hooks look superficially like crochet hooks, except that they have a wooden handle and that the rounded hook has an extra component, the latch (see diagrams). The latch opens when the hook is passed through the canvas and closes as it is pulled back again, forming the knot and bringing the pile to the right side.

The canvas used has no more than 10 holes to every 7.5cm/3in; any

Using the latch hook. 1 Wrap the piece of yarn around the shaft of the hook to give two ends of equal length. Continuing to hold the ends of yarn, push the hook down through a space in the canvas and back up through the adjacent space. 2 Pass the two ends of yarn through the open latch and tuck them down under the hook itself.
3 Pull the hook towards you so that the latch closes around the yarn. As you keep on pulling the ends will be drawn through the loop to complete the knot. 4 Before you move on to the next knot, check that this one is tight by giving the two ends of yarn a sharp tug.

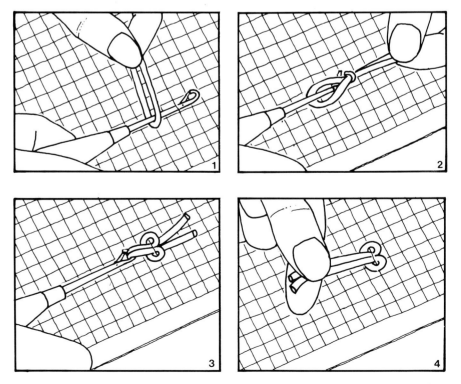

finer measure would be too small to allow the hook to pass through easily. For short-pile rugs special coarse 6-ply rug or Turkey wool is available in pre-cut lengths. However, rug makers often wish to cut their own wool – because they want to vary the height of the pile, perhaps, or for any of a number of other reasons. The simple formula they use is that the lengths of wool should be double the required height of the pile plus an extra 2.5cm/1in for the knot. Short-pile tufted rugs have a dense, hard-wearing surface and lend themselves to any style of design; however, because of the thickness of the yarn, they are not suitable for very intricate designs – for these gun tufting must be preferred.

The first stage in forming the knot is to fold the cut length of wool in half and loop it around the neck of the hook below the crook and latch. The cut ends of the wool are held in one hand while, with the other, the hook is pushed through a hole in the canvas and up through an immediately adjacent hole on the next row. The latch is opened manually and the two ends of wool are placed in the crook; then the hook is pulled back through the weave of the canvas. The latch closes automatically, pulling the ends of the piece of wool through the loop on the stem of the latch so that the knot is formed. The ends of wool are then pulled tight by hand so that the knot is made nice and firm. The work is done in rows across the canvas, a knot being made for each hole.

The same technique can be used to make one form of rya rug using cut lengths of wool, longer than for hand-tufting, to create a shaggy pile (see page 77 for a fuller discussion of rya rugs in general). A bundle of pieces of wool, all the same length but in different colours, is worked into a very coarse backing fabric and knotted using the latch hook. It is possible to buy the wool pre-cut, which saves considerable time-consuming effort. However, this restricts the range of colours available to the rug maker.

Gun-tufted Rugs

In a way, the technique of using a tufting gun to make rugs is unique. The product is without a doubt a hand-made rug, albeit one which requires the use of an automatic tool, yet it can hardly be described as a craft product since the technique involved has emerged not from traditional methods but from the technology used in industrial manufacture. The tool used, the tufting gun, is really nothing more than an advanced version of the carpet-repair gun used in industry to amend or repair machine-stitched carpets. Although the tufting gun available to the artist is still a fairly crude machine, it is now widely used in art schools and craft classes for experiment and tuition, while more and more rug makers are turning to it as a way of speeding the translation of their creative ideas into finished rugs.

The development of an industrial machine, the carpet-repair gun, into a craft tool available to the individual artist could not have been more timely. A few years ago the textile industry in Britain was very run down and the average student leaving school, college or university would have been very lucky indeed to find employment in the field. The outlook was made even grimmer by the fact that British industry was (and, for that matter, still is) little appreciative of the importance of design. Young artists looked to mainland Europe, where innovative design was welcomed, or started up their own workshops to produce their more experimental works — the works which we now see commanding high prices in the marketplace. All of this was true not only in the field of textiles, of course, but in any sphere where creativity and industry were supposed to complement each other, and did not.

In the creation of a gun-tufted rug, a vertical framework is set up to individual specifications in the workshop or studio. As the size of the framework obviously imposes limitations on the maximum size of rug that can be produced, the workshop should ideally have a very high ceiling. The framework should also be totally adjustable, so that smaller rugs can be made with the minimum wastage of canvas. The gun is held on a suspension unit, and this in turn is held from a roller bar fixed along the top of the framework, so that the gun can be moved freely both from side to side and up and down.

There are various different models of gun available. They run either on electricity or on a combination of electricity and compressed air, the compressed air being used to force the yarn through the shaft of the gun's hollow needle. For each tuft the gun is pushed forwards to puncture the canvas, which has been stretched tautly over the framework; the desired image is produced by manoeuvring the gun appropriately. The technique can be best described as rather like drawing or painting, except that, instead of a charcoal or paintbrush, one is using an electric needle loaded with wool.

The ease of manipulation of the gun offers considerable scope for individual expression, and this is precisely why the technique has since its earliest inception captured the imagination of creative rug makers. Using a tufting gun, you can create within a matter of weeks a rug very similar in quality to one which, if hand-tufted, would have required many months to produce. Moreover, because of the speed of production, it becomes much more practicable for the original designer to maintain full control throughout.

As with all rugs, the first stage in producing a gun-tufted rug is an idea — or at least the glimmerings of an idea. Different artists work in different ways, but many will put their idea down on paper to see how it looks (bearing in mind that it is going to be seen from every angle except straight-on, unless it is being designed as a wall-hanging). Alternatively, the image can be drawn in reverse directly onto the wrong side of the canvas — because, when using a tufting gun, one works from the back. More courageous artists skip the detailed design process and start with only the ''feel'' of an idea, working directly with the gun onto the canvas and improvising as they go along.

Opposite: ''Zip it Up'', a gun-tufted rug in pure wool by Malcolm Temple. Malcolm's geometric design in powerful primary colours is an object lesson in creating a sudden impact. The vibrancy of the two larger triangles is further heightened by the darkness of the central background, which is cleverly under- and overlaid by the intruding side-panel and, at the top, by the motif.

Assuming the maker has chosen to design the rug before starting work, he or she has to recognize the fact that the ideas are being put down on paper in two dimensions whereas the finished rug will of course be a three-dimensional object. The tufting gun is ideally suited to producing different pile heights in different areas of a single design. The tufts making up the pile can be made even or uneven, looped or cut, while at the same time up to four different coloured yarns can be used simultaneously – more if they are very fine. Similarly, the relative proportions of yarn used can be varied to create different textures and effects.

Gun tufting lends itself particularly effectively to abstract works which have bold flat areas of strong solid colour, notably alongside areas of texture which can be introduced either as a ground or in small selected areas of the design so that they act as highlights. The technique is very versatile, though, and there is no reason why it cannot be used equally effectively to produce more detailed figurative works. However, as with any textile art, it should not be forgotten that, if the technique is to be fully exploited as a way of turning an idea into its physical realization, the hand has to understand and appreciate the technique and the head the limitations of the medium.

The tufting gun has certainly had a very strong impact on the textiles field. As the tool itself continues to develop, so too do the styles and effects created by the artists who use it.

ABSTRACT AND GEOMETRIC DESIGNS

In order to illustrate the use of gun tufting to create abstract and geometric designs we shall concentrate on the work of Malcolm Temple. The striking primary colours and bold geometric shapes of his rugs are certainly not for the faint-hearted! His confident use of colour and authoritative sweep of design imbues all of his work with a directness that is as refreshing as it is energetic.

Malcolm originally studied painting at Wimbledon College of Art, London; although he still paints, the majority of his efforts are today focused in other directions. Over the years he has expanded his vocabulary to include the decorative as well as the fine arts, and has translated many of his ideas on colour, shape and form into a wide range of media, including theatrical design, sculpture, wood-carving, textile design and the design and construction of furniture. Whatever the medium he uses, the strong geometric and abstract patterns are evident throughout his work: a ceramic vase ripples with colour; an elegant candelabrum and steel chair contain a careful geometric rationale; *papier mâché* bowls combine texture and surface decoration.

However, nowhere are his ideas on design more immediately apparent than in his rugs. The gun-tufting technique allows him tremendous scope for transferring the hard-edged and often intricate shapes onto the rug canvas with absolute fidelity to the original concept. The rugs illustrated here bear witness to his passion for the vivid abstract works of such artists as Picasso, Kandinsky, Léger and

Opposite: Malcolm Temple's ''Slap'' is gun-tufted in pure wool. The design – in yellow, blue, black, orange, red and green surrounded by off-white – betrays the painter behind the designer. The shapes float on a red background framed by the off-white border, which is separate from but connected to the design by means of overlapping.

In this room setting we see Malcolm Temple's work in rug design used to its most dramatic effect in conjunction with other fruits of his labours. The rug, "Love Parade", is gun-tufted in wool, and uses his distinctive designs in strong primary colours.

Matisse — the masters of early-20th-century aesthetics and the people largely responsible for challenging and permanently changing our preconceptions of the very nature of art.

Insofar as it is possible to discern the influences on any maker's work, the choice of colours and the ways in which those colours are combined provide an identification as unique as, say, a fingerprint. The example of Malcolm's work shown on page 100 is no exception. The black background adds depth and provides a sharp contrast to the large blocks of strong colours. The rug is framed by a plain blue-grey border which further heightens the painterly feel of the overall design, with its flowing green, red, blue, yellow and orange shapes that delineate the design. The harmony is given to the overall effect by the yellow triangle, which both connects the shapes and relates them to each other.

Malcolm's colourful abstract rug designs are particularly suited to gun tufting. The close short pile of the tuft and the mode of action of the tufting gun allow the rug-maker to ''paint in'' the areas of different colour, finishing each in a precise line.

His designs for rugs are first worked out on paper, using as a starting point a shape that may be a symbol or a cypher for the whole design. In the case of ''Love Parade'', the red and blue shapes are sug-

Malcolm Temple's ''First Light'', gun-tufted in pure wool, is less rigidly geometric than some of his other works but nonetheless has a strong sense of colour and movement.

gestive of fertility symbols that are as old as the history of mankind itself; the sources of inspiration range from the earliest cave paintings to the so-called primitive art of West Africa and the South Seas, and then on to the Aztec art of Mexico. Malcolm himself regards his inspiration as having more to do with the Saxon and Celtic traditions, whether they take the form of the Sutton Hoo burial ship or an ornately jewelled Celtic cross.

Once he has roughed out his ideas in sketch form he begins to transfer his design onto another sheet, working to an approximate scale. He uses acrylics to paint in the shapes, experimenting with different colour combinations until he is satisfied. Acrylics give him an intensity of colour that is something of a trademark for him; he matches the original brilliance of the colours when he dyes the wool preparatory to making the rug.

Malcolm's rugs do undoubtedly have a dramatic effect, and therefore they need an assured and confident choice of furniture and soft furnishings, whose role is to complement and support the bald exhibitionism of the rug. Boldness can and does beget brilliance.

GALLERY OF DESIGNERS

Jennie Moncur

Jennie Moncur produces her interior furnishings working in a wide range of media and using a variety of textiles and techniques. The adaptable nature of the tufting process allows her to coordinate her designs down the walls, over chairs and onto the floor. In styling a complete room she applies her designs to different media, from painted fabrics to linoleum flooring; tufting enables the design of the rug accurately to reflect the room's overall style without any need for

Jennie Moncur's designs illustrate the tufted rug's ability to lend itself to precise patterns. The upholstery of the inlaid stool is covered with one of her tapestries, which shows a variation on the design of the rug.

Gun-tufted in pure wool, Jennie Moncur's "Flashback" rug, like much of her work, explores motifs and themes inspired by the art and architecture of the French Renaissance. Loose fleur-de-lys shapes contrast with the rich background, and the black and white triangles cutting across one corner give the hint of a border.

compromise. Another result of the technique's versatility is that, while some of her rugs hang on display in textile galleries, others are in full functional use.

Her prime inspiration has been the surface decoration she has observed in French Renaissance châteaux. Her work consequently explores pattern on pattern, combining different images while distorting their scale and perspective; she uses her rugs in conjunction with her complementary soft furnishings in order to further this end. Her carefully thought-out interiors, which aim to harmonize with the environment, likewise explore this interaction between different scales, surfaces and materials.

Liz Kitching

Architecture and the use of mosaics in it were what first inspired Liz Kitching's interest in floors and floor coverings. The use of wooden floors and ceramic and marble tiling, so much in evidence in traditional British design, is in fact a practice drawn from the countries of the European continent, which enjoy much warmer climates. Liz felt that these traditional methods needed to be adapted for the cooler temperatures of Britain, and tufted rugs were to provide an effective way of realizing the "warming" effect she had envisaged.

Because she tufts her rugs she is able to give equal importance to artistic content and practicability. Her design process starts with the collection of relevant images in various media – including photographs, drawings and rubbings – and then working in montage. In order to create the model colours, tones, solids and textures through which she can express her ideas, she paints countless pieces of paper

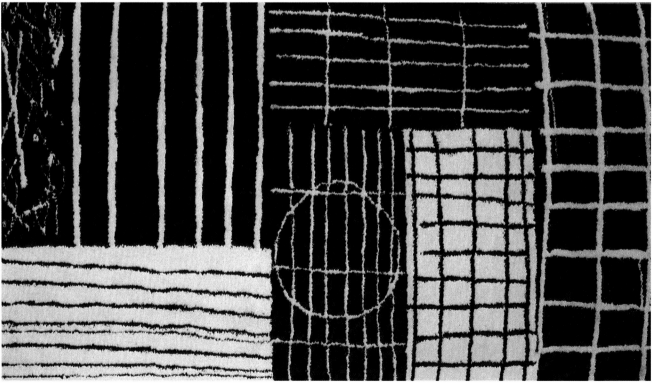

using acrylics, gouache and pastel. She cuts and places the papers and images, shifting the weight around until gradually she achieves the order and balance she desires. Once forms have started to suggest themselves, she completes them using drawn lines. She then considers colouring and pattern in terms of the depth of pile and density of texture she requires both to create the intended effect and to give the rug sufficient resistance to the wear and tear to which it is likely to be subjected.

Far top left: Ron Nixon's "postmodernist" gun-tufted rug for Mayfair Recording Studios. *Above*: This gun-tufted rug by Liz Kitching was especially designed for this interior. The way that the rug is overlaid with contrasting scrolled lines emphasizes the room's musical "feel". *Far left*: "Montage", another gun-tufted rug designed in black and white by Liz Kitching.

This gun-tufted wool rug by Liz Kitching is called "Miróesque No. 3", and, as the name suggests, Liz has drawn her inspiration directly from the work of the painter Joan Miró.

Lucy Clegg

Lucy Clegg's designs are bold, modern and colourful. She uses abstract shapes and strong primary colours in many of her rugs, and claims to draw much of her inspiration from Braque and Matisse. Lucy works with 80/20 carpet wool, and quite consistently to a pile depth of 18mm/$\frac{3}{4}$in. She produces rugs in a variety of shapes and sizes, working to commission.

Sandie Ennis

In 1986 Sandie Ennis formed Sandie Ennis Designs, a business specializing in hand-tufted rugs and wall hangings, as well as designs on paper for the fashion and furnishings industries. Sources for her dramatic rug designs include Ancient Egyptian drawings, North American Indian weaving and the tribal art of West Africa. Her

Lucy Clegg's gun-tufted rug, "Flying", has a dreamlike quality, as figures float in a black landscape.

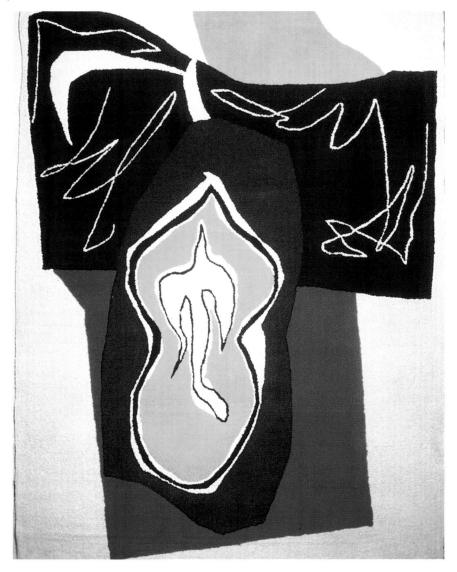

"Abstract 2", a gun-tufted rug by Lucy Clegg, was inspired by the work of Braque and Matisse. The bold design certainly conjures up 1950s imagery.

Above: A hand-tufted design by Sandie Ennis. Sandie has combined a simple colour scheme with a strong geometric design. *Right*: Again designed by Sandie Ennis, this hand-tufted rug, like the one above, uses simple colour tones. The design is inspired by Sandie's interest in African and North American Indian patterns.

Another hand-tufted rug designed by Sandie Ennis. This is a further stage in a series of rugs that explore the simple and uncluttered designs so often found in North American ethnic or tribal art. A brown earth tone has been added for warmth.

company's favourite designs involve an exploration of texture, tone and line using simple colour schemes in order to create original and vivid pieces of tufted work.

Celia Harrington

Celia Harrington travelled extensively in many parts of the world, living for a time in Trinidad, before settling in London and establishing her business as a designer and maker of one-off hand-tufted rugs.

As we have seen, one huge advantage of the tufting technique is that the finished rug can be made to accord very closely to any desired image and texture. To Celia this is the great attraction of the

The explosion of colour and movement that is a carnival in the West Indies provides the inspiration for this gun-tufted rug by Celia Harrington.

In this gun-tufted wool rug Celia Harrington's abstract shapes, in cream and black, repeat irregularly on a textured grey background.

medium. Many of her original ideas and concepts spring from things which she has seen while abroad, especially the annual carnival in Trinidad. Her slogan – "handmade by machine" – acknowledges the convenience and versatility which the assistance of modern tools has brought to traditional hand-tufting techniques.

She is a keen painter, and appreciates the way in which her work in tufting washes over into her paintings, giving them an additional vigour.

In this rug Celia Harrington has used gun tufting to create a painterly effect with splashes of colour and a dashed border.

Lynne Dorrien

Today Lynne Dorrien devotes most of her time and interest to producing hand-made rugs and wall-hangings. Her tufted rugs are made with 100 per cent wool and are generally strongly abstract in design, although her style also shows a preference for bold geometrics. Colour combinations are a very important consideration to her; her personal preference is often for black, while and grey (see pages

"Hopscotch" by Lynne Dorrien. This gun-tufted rug has a strong abstract design and a bold combination of colours.

119–20, where her work is further discussed). Her rugs are displayed in solo and group exhibitions all over the British Isles.

Gill Hewitt Barraclough

It is clear from Gill Hewitt Barraclough's bold rug designs that she has a colourfully painterly technique. Her works on paper are usually in mixed media, using texture to maximum advantage – just as she does in her gun-tufted rugs. Her images are inspired by her travels: she has visited North American Indian cultures and has journeyed in China and elsewhere in the Far East.

The gun-tufting technique allows Gill an enormous amount of freedom in translating her photographs and artefacts first into drawings and then to the finished rugs. She also furthers her enthusiasm by exploring and experimenting with the almost endless range

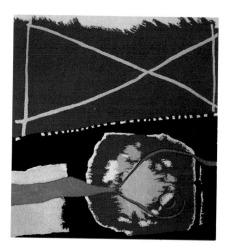

Far left: Gill Hewitt Barraclough's fine-art background is evident in this gun-tufted rug which, with its loose and colourful abstract design and its assured execution, "reads" just like a painting. *Left*: Another rug by Gill which looks just like a painting in wool.

113

Right: Gill Hewitt Barraclough's painterly technique is as evident in this rug as are the diverse exotic influences upon which she draws. *Opposite*: In black and white, Timney-Fowler's "Coinhead" rug is one of their many designs to have been inspired by neoclassicism. This influence appears also in their collection of dress and furnishing fabrics.

of textures and yarns that can be used with this technique. She finds that gun tufting is a comparatively rapid way of translating two-dimensional images into functional objects in a variety of shapes and sizes.

BLACK AND WHITE

The public image of the rug has been severely damaged by recollections of dingy, moth-eaten Victorian remnants dragged from dank attics. However, contemporary British rug-makers are doing much to sweep away this cobwebbed image of the role and function of the rug. A number of furnishing designers are effecting a compromise between British traditionalism and contemporary style by utilizing

the vivid contrast between black and white. In so doing they are bringing rugs out of a long Dark Age.

The best of today's rugs do not sentimentalize the past; instead, they are styled so that they marry the best of the past with the best of modern creativeness.

Timney-Fowler

Sue Timney and Graham Fowler are a married team committed to producing upmoded reproductions of images drawn from diverse cultural sources. Sue studied fine art and Graham fashion with textiles, both of them at the Royal College of Art, London. Since then they have built up an international reputation – first as freelance fabric designers known for their strong monochrome designs, and, more recently, as interior designers. Once upon a time they described themselves as ''20th-century vultures'': their inspiration is drawn from their travels and work in Japan, and their influences include Japanese prints, silk-screens and more general sources such as photography, mythology and classicism.

The results of their eclecticism can be seen in their rugs, furnishing fabrics, wallpapers, clothes, ceramics and accessories. Timney-Fowler's rugs, representing as they do the biggest enlargement of the images the couple have toyed with, are manifestly intended to be centrepieces. The Roman-style ''Coinhead'' rug (see photograph on page 115) is perfectly complemented by simple surrounds softened by curtains and drapes fashioned from fabrics designed in corresponding Roman patterns. Classical busts and images of Roman coins printed black-on-white round out the theme of the room.

Timney-Fowler's rugs are fully able to stand up for themselves without the addition of unnecessary colour. It is appropriate that they be photographed inside the couple's own West London house, as they are here. Such a house, situated on a main road, can be effectively removed from its urban ''mass-produced'' setting by styling its interiors in such a way as to conjure up images from different times and other places.

The playroom/dining-room downstairs in the Timney-Fowler house was originally two rooms, but is now a single room partitioned by large double doors. When the doors are open the central feature of the playroom, the ''Timepiece'' rug, is mirrored in the adjoining dining-room by a framed print of itself. Above the folding door is a Celtic-style frieze produced by the couple; a tablecloth, cushion-cover and crockery have been designed to echo the frieze. The playroom is used as such only occasionally but, when it is, a coordinating animal frieze finishes off this ''double room''.

The highly designed rug is great for large warehouse flats, adding a certain sense of grandeur to wide-open space and making a focal point of the feature rather than letting it be simply an apologetic attempt to make a large floor-space look smaller by adding gratuitous clutter. Timney-Fowler, in order to dramatize the setting yet further,

Opposite: Designed by Timney-Fowler, this gun-tufted rug coordinates with the black-and-white bedlinen and furniture.

offer a full range of Greek vases, Art Deco lamps and couture dress fabrics.

The Timney-Fowler "theme scheme" has attracted clients not only in Britain but also from other parts of the world. Among examples of overseas enthusiasm has been the Restaurant AD, in Tokyo, which called in these influential stylists to produce floor coverings which the client clearly regarded as being every bit as important as the other elements of room design. Now that there is a resurgence of classicism, today's individual tastes are being manifested on such a scale that even Roman-style atria are being used as focal points within building designs. Modern rugs can fit in harmoniously with this trend, blending an appreciation for the past with an awareness of the modern.

Lynne Dorrien

As we saw (page 111), Lynne Dorrien is a designer of hand-tufted rugs in 100 per cent wool. Her painterly achievements are remarkable in their looseness and versatility. She currently offers her collection, "Natural Rhythm", through retailers such as Mary Fox Linton and the Contemporary Textile Gallery, London. This collection has, too, been widely distributed to architects and interior designers, who place most of their orders on commission in response to the requests and/or requirements of their own clients.

The rugs in the "Natural Rhythm" collection — named after the first rug in the series — are predominantly black, white and grey, with occasional accents of red or turquoise. They provide perfect complements to settings of black, white and chrome. The "Natural

Opposite: Timney-Fowler's gun-tufted "Timepiece" rug boldly reflects the clockface in the background.

Below: This black-and-white design by Lynne Dorrien is part of a series based on simple lines and shapes.

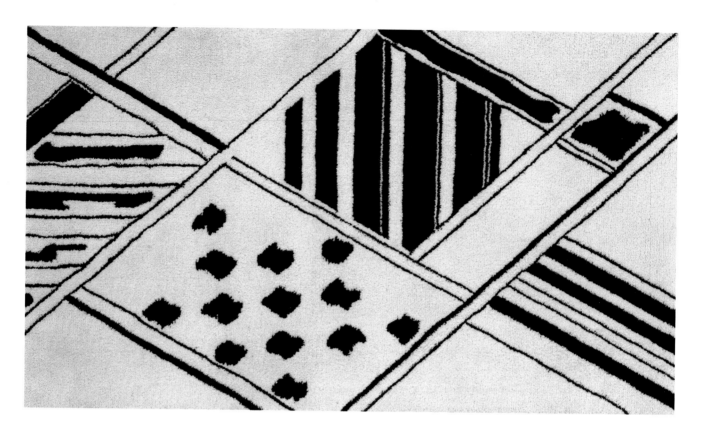

Another Lynne Dorrien design in the same series as the rug depicted on the preceding page.

Rhythm" designs can be produced in either black on white or *vice versa*.

Lynne works in several other media – painting, screen-printing, furniture restoration – and her geometric patterns and abstract designs are dramatic. However, the drama is kept well in place, so that her rugs seem perfectly at home even in traditional settings.

Her rugs have been selected for display with wall-hangings in exhibitions as diverse as "Art at Home" and the Crafts Council's "Top Office" show, as well as being selected for inclusion in the 1988 edition of *International Design Yearbook*. On a more permanent basis, her rugs are now featured also in art galleries, theatres, individual homes and a number of image-conscious offices. She has worked with the illustrator Brian Grimwood, who chose her to translate one of his ideas into a rug design; he felt that the result was as magnificent as anything in the Tate Gallery but had the advantage of being available to individuals and adaptable to personal requirements.

Although she admits that her personal preference is for designs in black, white and grey, Lynne acknowledges that, in rooms which have a generally monochromatic colour scheme, a coloured rug can be a vital element in creating a tone of softness and warmth. She therefore offers a plenitude of colour designs. To emphasize the larger, angled setting there is the "Cadillac" rug, which has her customary bold geometric pattern but the design is softened by waving and circular shapes. The effect is to moderate any tendency a room might have to become a repository of hostile and unyielding "design" objects.

PROJECT

A HAND-TUFTED RUG – "FISHES"

A hand-tufted rug with a Greek key border and using the ancient symbol of a fish. This black-and-white rug is simple in design and very easy to make.

You will need

- 190cm/75in × 150cm/60in canvas ($3\frac{1}{3}$ or 4 meshes per 2cm/$\frac{3}{4}$in)
- colour 1 rug yarn: 1.25kg/2lb 12oz in 5cm/2in lengths
- colour 2 rug yarn: 1.25kg/2lb 12oz in 5cm/2in lengths
- a latch hook
- a stout needle
- plenty of carpet thread or other strong thread
- 600cm/20ft rug binding

Method

Lay the canvas on a table with the selvedges at the sides. Count the squares (see chart on page 122) or draw the design from the chart onto the canvas. Before working the knots, turn over 4.5cm/1$\frac{3}{4}$in of canvas and work through this doubled canvas to form a finished end. Leave 5cm/2in at all edges before you begin knotting. Each square on the chart on page 122 represents one mesh of the canvas and one knot. Follow the diagrams on page 94 to make the knots. Using two strands of yarn, fold the yarn over the shank of the hook, holding the ends with your left hand. Keeping the hook in your right hand, hold the latch down with your index finger. Push the hook down through the mesh of canvas, under double horizontal threads, and up through the mesh above. Make sure the yarn is inside the hook when the latch closes, so that the end of the hook does not damage the yarn. Pull the hook back through the canvas, drawing the ends of the yarn through the loop. Tighten the knot by pulling the ends through your fingers, so that there are four tufts for each knot.

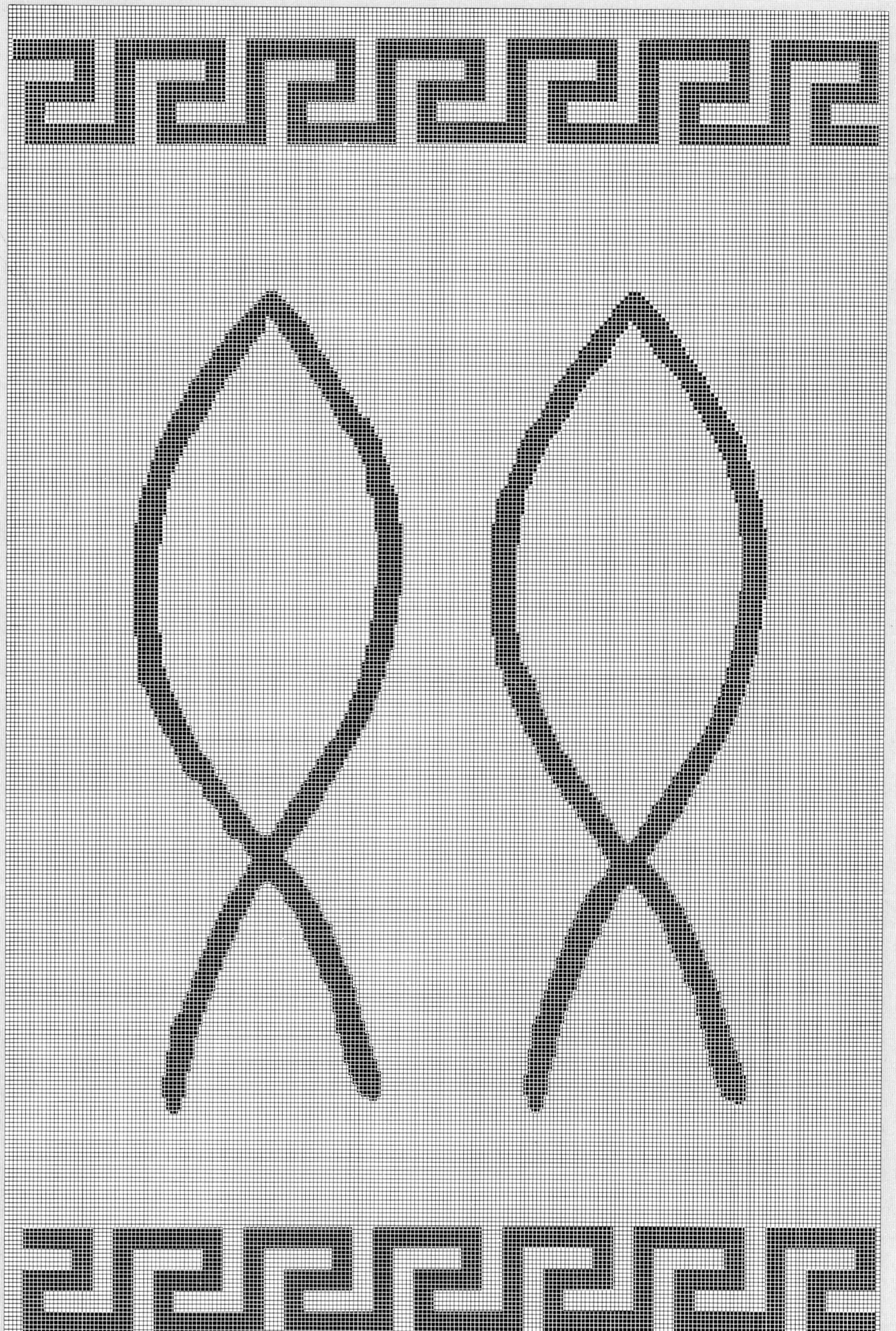

The yarn must be knotted on the weft threads (the threads running across the width of the canvas). To ensure even knotting throughout, work completely across the canvas before you start the next row. Alternatively you can risk knotting the design motifs first and then filling in the background: this certainly makes the work easier, but you have to be fairly confident about your ability to use even knots across the entire rug.

Change colours of yarn as you work across the canvas, following the chart as a guide. Work the rug up to just before 10cm/4in from the end. Turn up the 4.5cm/1¾in finished end and work the last 5cm/2in or so through doubled canvas, as at the beginning.

Once you've completed the main work, you need to finish the rug. Turn over the side edges (leaving selvedges on); slip-stitch these firmly to the underside of the rug using carpet thread (or other strong thread). Excess canvas at the selvedged sides can be basted in place on the underside of the rug.

Sew rug binding to the back edges of the canvas, stitching along both edges of the binding using carpet or other strong thread.

Opposite: The chart to follow for the hand-tufted rug, "Fishes."

Professional Tips

- If you feel sure that you will be able to use even knots all over the rug, save time by knotting the black areas first. Complete the fish motif and the Greek key border before you fill in the cream background.
- You might find it helps you to draw the design motifs (as worked out on your chart) directly onto the canvas. Use a felt-tipped pen for this. Once you've finished the rug the pen-marks will be invisible.

PROJECT

RUG BASED ON A DESIGN BY ZANDRA RHODES

This rug was created by Peggy King of Outsmoor Handcrafts, Camberley, UK. Its finished size is 130cm × 140cm/52in × 56in.

You will need
- a latch hook
- sufficient canvas with a weave of 10 holes to 7.5cm/3in
- wool – Readicut packs (each containing 320 cut strands): 39 blue, 28 light pink, 10 black, 11 white, 11 pale yellow, 3 deep pink
- a large needle
- strong thread or wool

The original needlepoint design by Zandra Rhodes which inspired this rug.

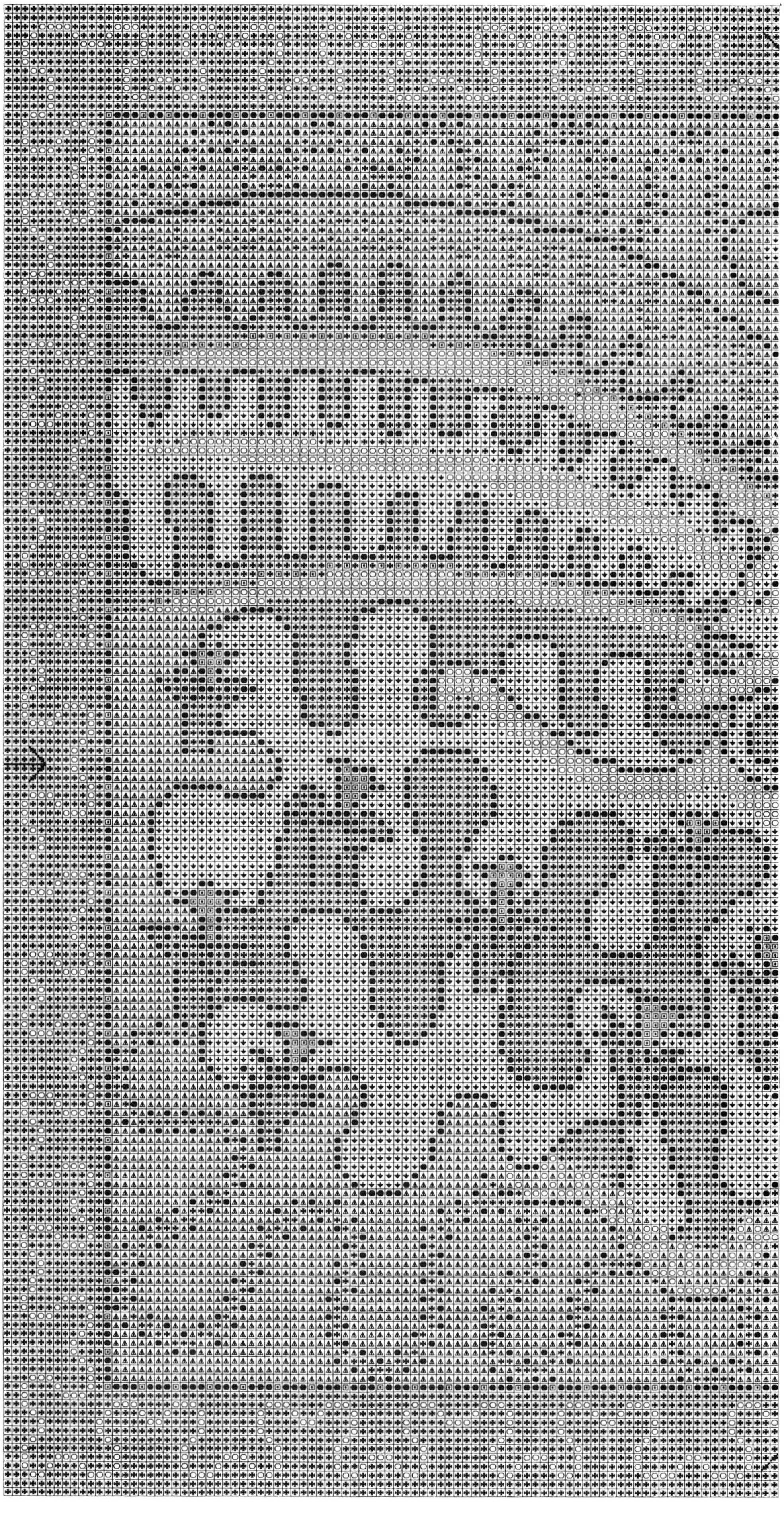

Key

- ● = black
- ✳ = blue
- ▣ = deep pink
- ▲ = light pink
- ✦ = pale yellow
- ○ = white

The chart to follow when making Peggy King's rug based on one of Zandra Rhodes's designs.

The finished rug, as made by Peggy King.

Method

Make sure that the canvas is larger than the finished size, so that you have enough left over to turn a hem once you have completed the rug. Using the cut wool, follow the diagrams on page 94 for knotting; use two strands for each knot. Start at the bottom left-hand corner and work each row at a time, changing colour as you go along.

Each square on the chart on pages 124–5 represents one hole of the canvas and therefore one knot.

To finish fold the hem to the back of the work and hem-stitch using a large needle and strong thread or wool.

Professional Tips

- The knotting of this rug is quite easy, but it takes quite a long time to make. Following the chart requires patience – but it's worth it.
- We have reproduced the chart to as large a size as we can. Nevertheless, if you find it too small to follow, see if you can get access to an enlarging photocopier.

7

NURSERY RUGS

The nursery is a haven from the bustle of the grown-up world, and it is here that one has one's earliest experiences of cosiness and security. From the toys on the floor to the colours of the pictures on the cot, the imaginative setting for a child's earliest bed-times is much more than simply a matter of blue walls for a boy and pink for a girl. As young children spend a great deal of time on the floor playing with their toys, thought must be given to its covering. Rugs are ideal, as they are hard-wearing, soft and warm and take up only part of the floor-space, leaving the rest of it free for rolling balls and pushing wheeled toys. And, as the baby or child is so much nearer the ground than most of us, the design on the floor is at least as important as that of the rest of the furnishings.

GALLERY OF DESIGNERS

McAdoo Rugs

McAdoo Rugs is a New England cottage industry producing bold and simple designs. The family makes 100 per cent virgin-wool hand-dyed and hand-hooked rugs. Strong on childlike unsophistication, the images are ideal for the nursery or playroom, no two rugs being identical, as the backgrounds are often improvised and styled to suit the individual.

The designs produced by McAdoo have their origins in traditional folk art and are inspired by sources close to the earth. Since many of their images are traditional in designs for children, it is easy to find coordinating soft furnishings. Among their themes are nautical designs with clipper ships, whaling scenes, native flora and fauna, polo players, dressage riders and country vistas. Obviously some of these are more suitable for children of a given age than others.

Flora and fauna are traditional folk-art subjects, and the ''New England Underwater'' rug shown here is a fine example of a naïve folk-art treatment. With lobsters, crabs, fish and bathing seagulls depicted in muted pinks, blues and greens, the rug paints a perfect picture of the mysterious world glimpsed in rock pools. It captures the freshness and fascination of one's very first visit to the seaside.

The ability of a rug like this to recreate one's earlier emotions can be enhanced if you select for the child's room fabrics, borders and mobiles presenting complementary themes. The room becomes not just the child's place of sleep and play but a complete environment, a private sanctum which is quite clearly distinct from the rest of the house. Here the rug suggests a room that is a mysterious underwater habitat, but with another rug one might create something quite dif-ferent – a forest hideaway, perhaps, or a grassy glade.

The North American tradition of hand hooking derives from early Scandinavian immigrants, who hooked cloth and bedcovers. The hand-hook looks rather like a steel crochet hook. The backing fabric has to have an open weave so that the yarn or fabric can be pushed

Opposite: This hand-dyed and hand-hooked rug by McAdoo is called ''New England Underwater''. It was inspired by the images of sea creatures, and is obviously ideal for a children's room.

Opposite: The circular "Starfish" rug has a coordinating appliquéd and embroidered fabric. This gun-tufted rug was designed by Luis Rivas Sanchez and made by Morgan & Oates. *Below*: A gun-tufted circular rug with a simple "duck" motif, designed by Nursery Times to coordinate with the surrounding fabric and wallpaper.

through. The method used is the same as that for the "Traditional Crazy Design with Scroll Border" hooked rug described on pages 50–2, the only difference being that, in place of the rags or strips of fabric, wool yarn is used.

Luis Rivas Sanchez

More abstract and highly designed, Luis Rivas Sanchez's "Starfish" rug, made by Morgan & Oates, is a more adventurous treatment of a marine theme. Rounding off the straight lines of the starker playroom walls, the edge of the "Starfish" rug is shaved and sculpted to add definition to the shape of the design.

Approximately 2m/6ft 6in in diameter, this rug is certainly dramatic. It is made by gun tufting wool onto a canvas base fabric, with woven raffia stitching used to pick out the starfish shape. When set in a room with the coordinating fabric that is available, the result is an adventurously intriguing source of wonder and a stimulant to the imagination of the enquiring child.

Nursery Times

Moving away from the aquatic theme we come to Nursery Times.

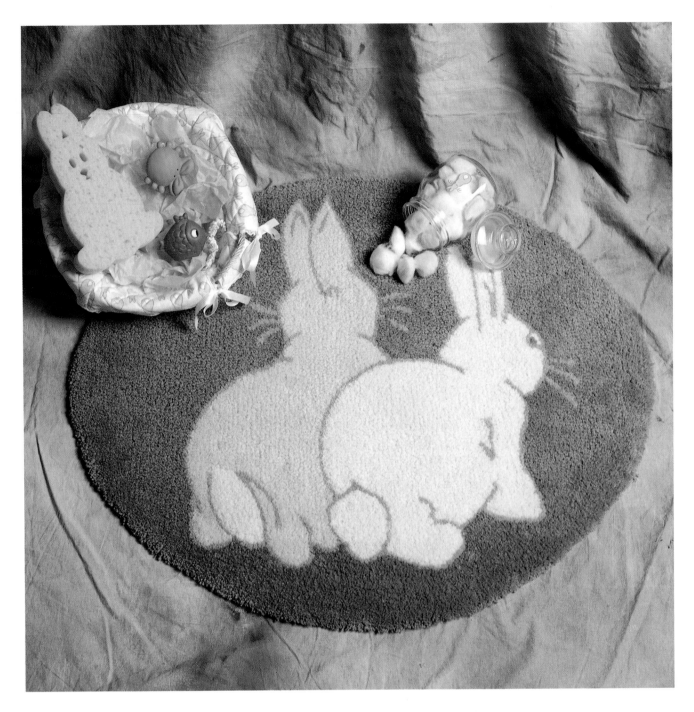

Another gun-tufted rug designed by Nursery Times for a children's room, this one uses pastel rabbits as its main theme.

This company produces simple, charming rugs whose designs reflect the preoccupations of childhood. Ducks and rabbits tread the pile of these gun-tufted rugs, which are made in 100 per cent wool. Matched with suitable fabrics and bordering for the walls or the skirting, these designs have the financially useful advantage of being able to sit harmoniously with many of the mass-produced furnishings available through department stores.

These rugs are on a manageable scale, and therefore simple designs can be hand-tufted. The design can be drawn onto the canvas, and the simple knotting technique required to achieve the tufts can easily be mastered by following the diagrams on page 94.

Readicut Wool Company

Fun and games are another integral part of the nursery – and what better than to put a game underfoot! Certainly there is no need to fold the "Snakes and Ladders" rug away at the end of the day. This rug, which is 90cm/3ft square, is made by the Readicut Wool Company in pure new wool worked using a full cross-stitch onto a five-mesh hand-stitched canvas.

The company produces a selection of other designs for children, featuring teddy bears, owls, robins, rabbits, mice and soldiers. Rabbits playing leapfrog or elephants teetering on a seesaw are among the many delightful subjects. Readicut's subsidiary, the Cartoon Carpet Company, produces similarly good-humoured subjects starring popular favourites from Mickey Mouse to the Thunderbirds.

An important point about the Readicut rugs is that they are avail-

Readicut Wool's "Snakes and Ladders" rug. This is a canvaswork rug made using cross stitch.

able in kit form so that adventurous parents can while away the evenings putting the rugs together themselves. The technique is not difficult: the lengths of wool are cut to measure, and they can be looped easily through the hand-stencilled, colour-coded canvas using the ingenious Readicut latch hook provided with the kit.

The specialist department of Readicut can create a pattern from virtually any photograph, so parents with ideas of their own can have a rug or rug kit customized especially to suit the mood they wish for their children's rooms.

GLOSSARY

Backing fabric The backing fabric is the foundation on which the rug is worked. Use the strongest backing fabric you can get hold of; if it wears out before the surface does you've wasted a lot of effort! It's a good idea, before you decide on your backing fabric, to experiment by working a small area.

Base fabric Often called backing fabric or ground fabric, the fabric onto which a rug is worked. Usually of canvas or hessian (burlap), although other materials (called warps) can be used instead.

Berlin woolwork A technique whereby coloured wools are woven onto canvas following a grid-like chart, in which each square represents one stitch.

Bias A line or cut across a fabric which is at an angle to the grain. A **true bias** is at exactly 45° to the grain.

Blocking Smoothing and squaring a finished piece of embroidery or tapestry by dampening it and pinning it out in shape until it is completely dry.

Bodkin A long needle with a large eye and a blunt edge.

Bolting cloth Cloth specially made for use as a base fabric in tapestry and so on. In theory it could be made from any type of fabric, but most usually synthetic fibres, cotton and linen are used.

Bouclé A type of yarn which has bumps or loops scattered hither and thither along its length.

Burlap A coarse, open-weaved fabric, sometimes known as hessian, made from jute and/or hemp. It is used as a base fabric in many rug-making techniques.

Canvas A coarse, loosely woven cloth widely used as a backing fabric. The warp and weft are woven so that the holes between the threads are precisely spaced in a regular grid. Various grid-sizes are available. *See also* Double canvas, Single canvas.

Canvaswork Any type of stitched work done on canvas, notably tapestry. The entire area is covered with stitching in various different styles. Embroidery on canvas is often called **needlepoint**.

Carding Brushing raw wool with fine wires to remove any tangles, impurities, etc. The resulting mass of fine strands can then be spun to produce yarn.

Counted-thread embroidery A technique whereby the positioning of each stitch is determined through careful counting of the warp and weft threads of the base fabric.

Double canvas Canvas in which the threads of the warp and weft have been woven in pairs. *Compare* Single canvas.

Dressing A stiffening agent often found in new fabrics. It is a mixture of starch, gum and size or china clay.

Embroidery A type of canvaswork (q.v.) which uses coloured threads or wools to produce a decorative effect, frequently but far from always pictorial.

Even-weave Term used to describe fabric which has a clearly defined mesh, whether the fibres have been woven singly, doubly or in higher multiples. Even-weave fabrics are useful for embroidery and tapestry only if the warp and weft threads are of equal thickness, as otherwise it is impossible to produce properly square stitches.

Felt A fabric made by deliberately matting together strands of wool (or other similar material) by mechanical action or, industrially, under the influence of heat and pressure.

Filling stitches Stitches used to fill a shape on the base fabric. They can be either small and densely packed, so that the shape is completely filled, or larger, so that a lacy effect is created.

Frame Any square or rectangular wooden framework which can be used to keep the base fabric taut while the work is in progress.

Frames can be as primitive as four pieces of wood nailed together or as sophisticated as some of the specialized versions available today. *See also* Slate frame.

Gauge The number of threads that can be stitched within a unit length (e.g., 2.5cm/1in) of backing fabric.

Grain The line of the warp. Working against (or across) the grain is simply working parallel to the weft.

Grounding stitches Stitches useful for covering large areas of background.

Ground fabric *see* Base fabric.

Hessian A coarse, open-weaved fabric similar to sackcloth, made from jute and/or hemp. It can be used as a base fabric.

Hooking Any of various techniques of rug making in which a hook is used to draw fibres or pieces of material through the base fabric.

Latch (latchet) hooking Hooking (q.v.) done using a hook which has a latch (or latchet), a bar which closes as the hook is drawn backwards so that the yarns or pieces of material do not become tangled.

Lining Rugs worked on stiff canvas do not need lining. If, though, you do need a lining, use a closely woven, heavy hessian piece which is 4cm/1½in larger all round than the finished size of the rug. Turn back the edges of unworked canvas to make a hem. Pin the lining to the back of the rug at intervals, starting at the centre and working outwards, making sure that the lining and the canvas have the same grains. Use a strong herringbone stitch to fix the lining to the canvas.

Maquette A small-scale model made before starting the main work.

Mitre A type of corner used when hemming a fabric. The ends of the two hems which meet at the corner are at an angle of 45° to the edge of the fabric. When they are folded over the result is a square corner. The term "mitre" is used also to describe the diagonal join so formed.

Nap The raised fibres of a piece of fabric – for example, velvet or tapestry work. If the nap all lies in a single direction, the colour of the surface will look different from different angles. If the nap lies any which way, the surface will look patchy, whatever the direction from which it is viewed.

Needlepoint *See* Canvaswork.

Pegging *See* Prodding.

Pile The yarns or pieces of cloth standing out from the base fabric. The term is used also to describe the length of one of these.

Plain-weave fabric Any fabric whose warp and weft threads are so irregularly woven that the fabric is useless as a grid for counted-thread embroidery (q.v.).

Prodding Often called pegging, a technique of rag-rug making in which the pieces of fabric are pushed through the base fabric using a blunt-pointed implement known as a prodder or peg.

Rolag A roll of soft wool which has been teased and carded, but which has yet to be spun.

Rya rugs Rugs in which bundles of yarns are together stitched or hooked onto the base fabric.

Scrim A fine, open-weave canvas which used to be made from low-grade linen but which now is likely to be of cotton or a mixture of fibres. Generally light brown in colour, it can be used as a base fabric.

Single canvas Canvas in which the warp and the weft have been woven in single threads. *Compare* Double canvas.

Slate frame Wooden frame which has two rollers and two side-pieces slotted at their ends to take the rollers. The rollers have webbing attached to them; to this webbing the ends of the base fabric are stitched while the work is in progress. Down each of the side-pieces is a row of holes through which pegs can be put. Adjustment of the pegs controls the tension in the fabric.

Slub A yarn which has random thick and thin sections along its length, due to uneven spinning. It can be used to effect in weaving to give a knobby texture to the finished work.

Soft cotton A five-ply thread, tightly twisted and with a matt finish.

Stranded cotton A six-ply thread, loosely twisted and slightly shiny. The threads can be separated for use in twos or threes.

Tapestry A form of canvaswork (q.v.) in which coloured threads are woven onto a fixed base fabric (q.v.).

Tapestry needle A long, broad, blunt needle with a large eye.

Tapestry wool A four-ply wool frequently used in canvaswork.

Thrums Scraps of yarn left over from the commercial manufacture of carpets. These scraps can be used by rug makers. Typically they come in bundles containing a random mixture of coloured strands.

Tramming Preparing double canvas (q.v.) so that the final stitched surface will be harder-wearing. Before the decorative work begins, horizontal straight stitches in colours that accord with the design are worked between the canvas threads. When the decorative stitches are worked over these they are filled out. Tramming also makes it easier to fill in areas of background.

Tufting A generic term for a number of rug-making techniques in which yarns or pieces of fabric are knotted onto the base fabric.

Tufting gun A device which can be bought by manual rug makers and used to increase vastly their rate of tufting.

Warp The threads running in the lengthways direction of the weaving loom. The weft (q.v.) threads are woven at right angles through them.

Warp (fabric) *See* Base fabric.

Weft The threads running across the width of the weaving loom. They are woven at right angles through the warp (q.v.) threads.

Suppliers

United Kingdom

Equipment

Mary Allen
Wirksworth
Derbyshire

Atlantis Art
Gullivers Wharf
105 Wapping Lane
London E19 1RW

Bits and Bobs
18 Lodge Road
Holt
Wimborne
Dorset

Camden Needlecraft Centre
High Street
Chipping Camden
Gloucestershire

Candlemakers' Supplies
28 Blythe Road
London W14 0HA

L. Cornelissen & Son
105 Great Russell Street
London WC1B 3RY

Craftsmans Mark Ltd
Trefnant
Denbigh
North Wales

A.S. Cumming & Co.
Unit D6
Princesway North
Team Valley Trading Estate
Gateshead
Tyne & Wear

Ann Davies
1 Wingrad House
Jubilee Street
London E1 3BJ

de Denne Ltd
159–61 Kenton Road
Kenton
Harrow
Middlesex

Dryad (Reeves) Ltd
PO Box 38
Northgates
Leicester

Dylon International Ltd
Lower Sydenham
London SE26 5HD

Christine Ellis
'R Efail
Tir Stent Bach
Dolgellau
Gwynedd

Emmerich (Berlon) Ltd
Wotton Road
Ashford
Kent

Green Bros Ltd
Summerheath Road
Hailsham
East Sussex

William Hall & Co. (Monsall) Ltd
177 Stanley Road
Cheadle Hulme
Cheadle
Cheshire

Handweavers Studio & Gallery Ltd
29 Haroldstone Road
London E17 7AN

Harris Looms Ltd
Northgrove Road
Hawkhurst
Kent

Frank Herring
27 High West Street
Dorchester
Dorset

Kemtex Services Ltd
Victoria Works
Wilton Street
Denton
Manchester

Lervad (UK) Ltd
18 Vernon Buildings
Westbourn Street
High Wycombe
Buckinghamshire

John Maxwell
Folder Lane
Burgess Hill
Sussex

Jennifer Page
Ashurst Cottage
Birchwood
Near Malvern
Worcestershire

Royal School of Needlework
25 Princes Gate
London SW7

Neville Smith
Penfillan Spinning Wheels
Keir
Thornhill
Dumfries

Whaleys (Bradford) Ltd
Harris Court
Great Horton
Bradford
West Yorkshire

Yarn
Anglia Fibres Ltd
Lady Lane Estate
Hadleigh
Ipswich
Suffolk

A.K. Graupner
Corner House
4 Valley Road
Bradford
Yorkshire

J. Hyslop Bathgate & Co.
Victoria Works
Galashiels
Selkirkshire

H. & J. Jones
58 Wood Street
Liverpool

Mace & Nairn
89 Crane Street
Salisbury
Wiltshire

Hugh MacKay & Co. Ltd
PO Box 1
Dragonville Trading Estate
Durham

Rowan Yarns
Washpit
Holmfirth
West Yorkshire

Seba Lace
76 Main Street
Addingham
Ilkley
West Yorkshire

Shades
57 Candlemas Lane
Beaconsfield
Buckinghamshire

Silken Strands
33 Linksway
Gatley
Cheadle
Cheshire

Somic Ltd
PO Box 8
Alliance Works
Preston
Lancashire

J. & W. Stuart Ltd
Esk Mills
Musselburgh

Texere Yarns
College Mill
Barkerend Road
Bradford
West Yorkshire

Textilose Ltd
Mosley Road
Trafford Park
Manchester

Weavers' Shop
Royal Carpet Factory
Wilton
Near Salisbury
Wiltshire

Fabric
Liberty of London
Regent Street
London W1

MacCulloch & Wallis
25–6 Dering Street
London W1

George Weil & Sons Ltd
63–65 Ridinghouse Street
London W1P 7PP

Kits
Erhman
Vicarage Gate
London SW7

J.R.C. Handicrafts
Croft Mill
Hebden Bridge
West Yorkshire
HX7 8AD

Readicut Wool Co. Ltd
Terry Mills
Ossett
West Yorkshire
WF5 9SA

Beads
Ells & Farrier
5 Princes Street
London W1

Places to Visit
The American Museum in Britain
Claverton Manor
Bath

Shipley Art Gallery
Prince Consort Road
Gateshead
Tyne & Wear

USA and Canada

Equipment
J. & P. Coats (Canada) Inc.
Station A
PO Box 519
Montreal
Quebec

Gilmore Looms
1023 North Broadway Avenue
Stockton
California

LeClerc Industries
PO Box 267
Champlain
New York State

The Looms
Far End
Shake Rag Street
Mineral Point
WI 53565

Macomber Looms
PO Box 186
Beech Ridge Road
York
Maine 03909

L. W. Macomber
166 Essex Street
Saugus
Massachusetts

Norwood Looms
505 S. Division Avenue
PO Box 167
Fremont
Michigan 49412

Yarn
Susan Bates
212 Middlesex Avenue
Chester
Connecticut

The Batile and Weaving Supplier
393 Massachusetts Avenue
Arlington
MA 02174

Classic Yarns
12 Perkins Street
Lowell
MA 01854

Conlin Yarns
PO Box 11812
Philadelphia

DMC Corporation
107 Trumbull Street
Elizabeth
New Jersey

Fort Crailo Yarn Co.
2 Green Street
Rensselaer
New York State

Frederick Fawcett Inc.
1304 Scott Street
Dept FA
Petaluma
CA 94952

Greentree Ranch Wools
163 N Carter Lake Road
Loveland
Colorado

Johnson Creative Arts
445 Main Street
West Townend
Massachusetts

Old Mill Yarn
PO Box 115
Eaton Rapids
Michigan

Webs
PO Box 349
18 Kellog Avenue
Amherst
MA 01004

The Wool Gallery
1555 Fir Street
Salem
OR 97302

Woolstons Wool Shed
651 Great Road
Bolton
MA 01740

The Yarn Basket
2723 Coltsgate Road
Dept F
Charlotte
NC 28211

The Yarn Depot
545 Sutter Street
San Francisco
California

The Yarnery
1648 Grand Avenue
St Paul
Minnesota

Other Suppliers

Belding Corticelle 1982 Inc.
617 Denison Street
Markham
Ontario

Earth Guild
One Tingle Alley
Dept FA
Asheville
NC 28801

Slevers
Fox Lane
Washington lse
WI 54246

The Weavers Knot
Dept FA
121 Cleveland Street
Greenville
SC 29601

The Weavers Store
11 South 9th Street
Columbia
MO 65201

Europe

Equipment

Loom Company Varpapuu
76120 Pieksamaki
Finland
(exported by Oy Varpa Looms Ltd
Osmontie 35
46800 Myllykoski
Finland)

Yarn

Bernheim et Fils
33 Rue de Jeuneurs
Paris
France

Fokeningen Hemslojden
Box 433
Boras
Sweden

Helmi Vuorelma OY
Vesijarvenkatu 13
15141 Lahti 14 Pl. 45
Finland

Norsk Kunstvevgarn
Hombursand
pr Grimstad
Norway

Schachenmayr
Mann & Cie Gmbh
Postf 1160
D-7335
Salach
West Germany

Kits

Svenska Readicut
1 Kungsbacka A-B-
Verstadsgaten 14
43400 Kungsbacka
Sweden

Australia and New Zealand

Equipment and Yarn

Coats Patons (New Zealand)
48–52 Wyndham Street
Auckland 1

Coats Semco
Semco Park
8A George Street
Sandringham
Victoria 3192
South Australia

Kits

Readicut Australia
PO Box 117
Mitcham 3132
Victoria

Other Suppliers

Olivier (Australia) Pty Ltd
47–57 Collins Street
Alexandria
New South Wales

Warnaar Trading Co.
376 Serry Road
PO Box 10567
Christchurch

INDEX

Figures in *italics* refer to the sites of relevant captions.

ACKNOWLEDGEMENTS

It would be impossible to acknowledge everyone who has helped in the creation of this book. However, a few people deserve special thanks. Among them are: Ray McNeill, Nat McNeill, *Pins and Needles*, Jeanette Harrison of the Contemporary Textile Gallery, Sally Lines, Alex Kirri, Shipley Art Gallery, Ariadne, Zandra Rhodes, Julia Milne, Timney-Fowler, Andrew Sydenham, India Wadsworth, Sarah Charles, Monique Le Luhandre, Don Wales, Chris Taylor.